PRO...

David Freemantle's first b... ...estselling *Super-boss*, was widely acclaimed and has been translated into ten languages around the world. In addition to writing he runs a thriving international consultancy practice aimed at helping organizations achieve individual managerial excellence.

Prior to taking up writing and consultancy he pursued a successful career in management, culminating as a Board Director of British Caledonian Airways.

To: Peter

Best wishes

every success

David Freemantle

24/2/89

Dedication
Ruth Elena

David Freemantle

PROFITBOSS

PAN BOOKS
in association with
Sidgwick & Jackson

First published in Great Britain 1987 by Sidgwick & Jackson
This edition published 1988 by Pan Books Ltd,
Cavaye Place, London SW10 9PG
in association with Sidgwick & Jackson
9 8 7 6 5 4 3 2 1
© David Freemantle 1987
ISBN 0 330 30416 X
All rights reserved

Printed and bound in Great Britain by
Richard Clay Ltd, Bungay, Suffolk

Contents

Acknowledgements

I would like to thank my wife Mechi for all her encouragement as well as practical help in writing this book. I also wish to thank Joanna Edwards and Robert Smith for the valuable inputs they have made in preparing the final version.

Introduction

Profit! It's always on the mind of a Profitboss except perhaps when making love, growing roses or sailing through storms. And even then on occasions.

He (it could be she) is obsessed with profit. So are his people. The Profitboss thinks 'profit' all day long. Every decision he makes, every action he takes, every word he utters is geared to profit.

What's more, on nine days out of ten he makes profit. On the tenth day he learns a little more and that's why he's still in business, whether as a warehouse supervisor, a drug-store manager, a publishing executive, a manufacturing director or the president of an insurance company.

The Profitboss never allows himself to get stifled by the suffocating systems of an overheated, overmanaged and overmanned organization. Bureaucracy is the bane of his life. If a personnel guy sticks a performance appraisal form in his face he'll ask: 'How can I profit from this?' And if the personnel guy can't answer sensibly, the Profitboss will find a more sensible use for that particular piece of paper.

The Profitboss achieves profit in any way he can. He'll be an opportunist one minute, an entrepreneur the next and an achiever a few seconds later. But he will never stop being a leader.

He might be held out to be a hard-nosed whizz-kid who railroads his ideas through the complaining conservatives of an overcautious company, but in the end he knows he cannot achieve profit without the support of his people. The Profitboss cares for his people. He cares for them so much he'll fire any team-member who doesn't contribute to profit.

It's as simple as that. The Profitboss is not going to let his eye off the ball by wasting time on losers. Nor will he waste his time attending committee meetings and arguing about the price of baked beans in the staff restaurant. Nor will he be distracted by the debilitating deliberations of certain union people and the distrust they ferment.

The Profitboss keeps the accent on the positive. He knows how to invest his time and energy profitably, and often that means investing in people – choosing them, paying them, developing them.

The Profitboss delivers, not just because the company has the right products and services, but because he has an attitude of mind to deliver. And that takes 'believing'. This book is all about that attitude of mind, the associated 'beliefs' and how the Profitboss puts them into practice on a minute-by-minute basis day by day. It is based on over twenty years' experience and personal study as to why some bosses throughout any organization are much more successful at contributing to profit than others.

The Profitboss is, of course, a Superboss, and the range of practices described here complement those in my previous book.* They are by no means exhaustive nor comprehensive, and to that extent the book can be dipped into on a 'page-a-day' basis, as with *Superboss*. Investing five minutes or so in reading one or two of the following pages might be the most profitable thing you've done for a long time. And if you read the whole book – well! The world is your oyster!

* *Superboss*, (Gower Publishing Company Limited, 1985).

1
THE PROFIT CHALLENGE

The profit attitude
The profit philosophy
The profit strategy
Profit leadership
Profit priorities
Power and profit
Innovation for profit

The profit attitude

Profit is an attitude of mind

The eyes of a Profitboss focus only on profit.

It is an obsession with him. He sees profit in every business situation. He seeks a profitable opportunity every second of the working day.

Dedication to making profit is an attitude of mind which the Profitboss instils throughout his organization. He makes it a way of life. It is something his people never stop working for.

- The Profitboss sees no profit in breaking the law. Nor bending it.

- The Profitboss sees no profit in treating his people badly. Nor their union.

- The Profitboss sees no profit in neglecting his customers. Nor suppliers.

- The Profitboss sees profit in ensuring that his people have excellent working conditions.

- The Profitboss sees profit in ensuring that his fleet of delivery vehicles is modern, well-maintained and clean-looking.

- The Profitboss sees profit in paying his people well.

- The Profitboss sees profit in every business contact he makes.

- He sees profit in speaking at conferences, replying promptly to customer queries and being genuinely polite to all he meets.

- He sees profit in the way the receptionist smiles and the way the telephonist answers a call.

- He sees profit in the demeanour of his secretary and how she manages the filing system.

- The Profitboss sees profit at 8.00 in the morning when he drives into the car-park and at 6.00 in the evening when he leaves for home.

- The Profitboss sees profit in every single person in the organization.

When you see a Profitboss, you see profit.

TODAY'S STEP

What is your attitude?

Get out the microscope (your eyes, your ears) and examine in detail every decision you make, every word you say and every action you take today.

Clarify your profit objectives for each decision, word and action. If you can't do this, question the reason. Why bother if there's no profit in it?

If you decide to visit Linden House next Tuesday, evaluate that decision in terms of profit.

If you write a memo to Charlene Vickers, evaluate that memo in terms of profit.

If you take action on the Gold Star issue, evaluate that action in terms of profit.

At the end of the day put the microscope away and assess how much profit you've made for the company in the previous twenty-four hours. If it doesn't cover your salary, you know what to do.

REMEMBER

The PROFITBOSS profits through people, not at their expense.

The profit philosophy

Making profit requires philosophy

You have a choice. You can let your destiny control you, or you can control your destiny.

If you choose the former course, you will be one of the majority who react to situations and never take the lead. The animal instinct will prevail. To achieve the latter you need a philosophy.

The Profitboss has a clear philosophy for managing people for profit. It is a philosophy he has successfully evolved over the years and which embraces a whole spectrum of principles, beliefs, values, attitudes and perceptions. It is a philosophy which relates the company to customers, people to profit, and competition to compassion. It is a philosophy which can be practically implemented every minute of the working day.

It is a philosophy geared to making profit and achieving excellent results, a philosophy based on a humanitarian and benevolent approach to managing people, a philosophy based on mutual respect, dignity, trust and co-operation.

The philosophy of a Profitboss is always clear, so that he can communicate it to his people to get their support and commitment. It is a framework which yields up opportunity and closes off ambiguity. The clear philosophy of a Profitboss facilitates his actions, his decisions, his behaviour on a daily basis, eliminating doubt and demonstrating conviction.

TODAY'S STEP

Do you have a philosophy?

Take a long stroll across the park at lunch-time. Think very carefully about your philosophy of leadership, management and business. Think very carefully about your philosophy for making profit. Try to summarize in your mind its key points.

When you get home tonight, find a quiet hour away from the television and family and jot down on paper the key points of this philosophy.

For each point in your philosophy try to identify the action you have taken today (and will take tomorrow) which effectively puts this philosophy into profitable practice.

REMEMBER

There is no wiser a philosopher than the PROFITBOSS.

The profit strategy

Strategies should be mind games, not paper exercises

Most people don't know what a strategy is. This includes most strategic planners.

The management world is full of strategic direction, strategic objectives, strategic goals, strategic action plans and strategic strategies. It is also full of people who never implement the strategies they spend months devising.

Strategies are useless unless the key points can be summarized in a few lines and committed not only to memory but also to real action.

An effective strategy is the clear route to a profitable 'vision of success'.

The Profitboss has his own personal 'vision of success'. It is encapsulated in a few key phrases, for example: 'The highest-quality standards in the industry'; 'The fastest and most efficient customer service'; 'Excellent employee relations'. He has clearly defined ways of realizing this vision: financial, manufacturing and marketing. These are ways which involve every member of his team. That's his strategy and it's always in his mind.

The Profitboss doesn't waste valuable time producing detailed data for 100-page draft strategies produced by sycophantic strategic planners to fill out filing cabinets. The process always comes to nothing because nobody will remember what's in the strategic plan and nobody will commit to it. In any event, everything will change tomorrow.

Effective strategy cannot be the product of a bureaucratic system. For the Profitboss effective strategy is the way forward to realizing the 'vision of success' he has in his mind. It's that simple.

TODAY'S STEP

Have you prepared your strategy?

Spend five minutes summarizing your personal strategy for success for your own area of responsibility and relate this to company strategy. If you can't do this, you have no strategy and are unlikely to be successful.

Destroy those 100-page strategy documents carefully locked away in the filing cabinet – you never look at them anyway. Better still, send them to your business competitors: that will really put them off the scent! (On second thoughts . . . !)

REMEMBER

The PROFITBOSS produces profit from action, and action from strategy.

Profit leadership

The difference between a manager and a leader is the measurable profit achieved through people

The title 'manager' should be abolished. It has become all things to all people – all things, that is, except leadership. Administrators are managers, senior professionals are managers, every Pam, Nick and Gary is a manager. But few are leaders. The titles 'director' and 'vice-president' are in danger of going the same way too.

The Profitboss rises above his assigned management role to become a leader. Whatever the dictates of the corporation, whatever the pressures from the union, the Profitboss sees his role essentially as leading a team of people in pursuit of his profit goals.

He doesn't let other people take the lead for him, having no truck with the Personnel Department if they try to take the reins out of his hand, nor the union if they try to do the job for him.

As a leader the Profitboss believes he is accountable for his team. No one else has that accountability. It is an accountability for developing a trusting, caring relationship within the team – caring for high performance.

As a leader the Profitboss is perfectly clear about his 'vision of success' and the essential requirement of securing the co-operation and commitment of his team to realizing that vision. It is a process that cannot be administered or managed by corporate policy or the application of personnel systems. It is essentially a personal process pertaining to the relationship between a boss and his people.

To that extent the achievement of profit through good leadership is also very much a personal thing. It is this personal leadership element which distinguishes the Profitboss from administrators and other so-called managers.

TODAY'S STEP

Are you a leader?

Whether you manage one person or a thousand, assess the degree to which you have established yourself as a leader in the pursuit of profit. Answer these questions:

- Do you see your role just as an administrator, a 'postbox', a 'telephonist' or a 'committee member'? Many managers do.
- In what way have you personally taken command of your team?

  Do you command their respect?
  Do you command their loyalty?
  Does this command generate trust?
- Do you take the lead in developing shared, profit-oriented goals with them?
- Do you show genuine appreciation for their individual contributions?
- Have you led your team through a co-operative approach and gained their total commitment to achievement of your profit goals?

To qualify as a leader it is essential you answer 'yes' to all but the first question.

Having carefully assessed your leadership position today, take some immediate action to develop yourself further as the leader of your team. (For example, buy everyone lunch and 'chew the cud' for half an hour.)

REMEMBER

The PROFITBOSS is a profit-leader.

Profit priorities

Profit should be your last priority

The people who earn you the profit should be your top priority. If you make them your lowest priority, there will, in the long term, be no profit.

Profit is an attitude of mind, not a priority. The priority is to develop that attitude in your staff, to convince them that they are the key generators of profit, that they have the biggest contribution to make. It is they who sell for profit, not the Profitboss. It is they who produce for profit, not the Profitboss. It is they who are the Profitboss's biggest priority – along with the other people who count: the customers.

Because customers are people, the Profitboss gives priority to establishing and maintaining effective relationships with them. The Profitboss is therefore always re-ordering his priorities to meet the needs of his customers and his people.

If Ken Kingsley at Christie's has an urgent requirement, the Profitboss will give priority to Ken rather than devote his time, as scheduled, to completing the budget. If Jan Miller needs an urgent decision, he'll give priority to Jan rather than spend time at his desk completing the sales plan. That will come later, along with the budget. If both Ken and Jan need him at the same time, he will have to choose which should take priority, a decision he'll explain to Jan when he sees her at 1.50pm.

TODAY'S STEP

How high are your people priorities?

Take a sheet of paper and draw four columns. Head each column as follows:

Column 1   TODAY

Column 2   THIS WEEK

Column 3   THIS MONTH

Column 4   THIS YEAR

Now list your top three priorities for each category, for example, first of all, setting up the 'away day' for your team you've been postponing for months.

Analyse the list. How many of the twelve priorities are 'people' priorities? If the answer is nine or more, you are a Profitboss. If the answer is three or less, you are probably an unmitigated management disaster and should transfer to accounts.

REMEMBER

The person with the biggest problem has the highest priority for the PROFITBOSS.

Power and profit

No one person has the power to make profit

Power is a negative concept. Everyone has the power to stop you doing things, to get in the way of making profit. Your customers have such power. Your suppliers have such power. Your employees have such power.

You have no power to profit from your customers, suppliers or employees. At best you have the power of persuasion, but you have no power (in this day and age) to impose decisions, to force the achievement of profit. Such force, in an earlier age, would have been called exploitation. Today such force is a dead loss.

Many managers delude themselves that they have such power. But they have only the power to stop things happening, not to make them happen.

Real power to make profit lies in a co-operative effort – a co-operative effort between the company and customers, between managers and employees. The Profitboss harnesses such power, a power adduced from the efforts of the people he works with (including his clients). He needs no other power.

Individual power corrupts, creates abuses. So does corporate power. If a company believes it has the power to force a supplier into submission, such power will corrupt. If a company believes it has the power to restrict employees' pay to an unacceptable level, that power will create abuses.

Power is a concept that is not prevalent in the Profitboss's thinking, nor in his vocabulary.

TODAY'S STEP

What positive powers do you really have?

Examine your relationship with other departments in your company, with people in your own department, with external contacts, with people above you in the hierarchy. What positive powers do you have over them?

What positive power do you have to make a profitable contribution to the company?

Now examine closely your negative powers, the power to control expenses, to stop recruitment, to resist training, to fail to co-operate either actively or passively.

Establish where your power to achieve profit really comes from. Is it ascribed to you by your boss? Or does it really come from the co-operative efforts of the people you work with?

Identify one powerful way today to further harness the power of such co-operative effort.

REMEMBER

The only power a PROFITBOSS has is that of the people around him.

Innovation for profit

Innovation is the source of all profit

In a world where everything is changing it is far more profitable to initiate change than react to it.

Innovation is the creative accomplishment of such change. Profit stems from the controlled support of the innovative process in an organization. The process is complex because one single creative idea from, say, a junior executive will get nowhere unless it is championed by others.

The Profitboss champions innovators. He gets the necessary support from his team, his colleagues, his board, his union for any innovation pioneered by his people. But the innovation must have profit potential and he must be convinced of that.

The last thing the Profitboss does is reject a new idea out of hand because he didn't think of it in the first place, or because it's too much trouble. Unfortunately, it's something many executives do. With their closed minds they give little thought to new ideas put forward by their people, often dismissing their suggestions as 'silly', 'ill-considered' or 'unrealistic'. The jet-plane was similarly classified when first thought of.

The Profitboss listens carefully, keeps an open mind and, when convinced, will nurture, foster and champion innovative ideas, whether it be Sally Unwin's new strategy for product marketing, Carol Reed's new system for fuel saving, Hilary Smith's new approach for handling customer complaints or Tony Tucker's new system design.

Encouragement, energy and commitment are the key qualities the Profitboss shows in supporting the innovative process.

TODAY'S STEP

Is innovation a part of your style?

Take two innovative steps today.

The first should be to identify and evaluate (in terms of profit) the main innovations you have championed during the last year.

The second is to get your team to generate at least two innovative ideas for further improving profit. Sit down with your people at lunch-time and do some brainstorming.

Make a list of all innovative ideas, no matter how crazy, and then select the two which show the most 'profit potential'. Ensure you get commitment to the follow-through.

REMEMBER

The PROFITBOSS champions innovators.

2

ESSENTIAL QUALITIES IN THE PROFITBOSS

Vision
Belief in product
Risk-taking ability
Professionalism
Knowledge of facts
Decisiveness
Uniqueness
Openmindedness
Courtesy
Consistency
Service-orientation
Focus on end-results
Conviction to the point of resignation

Vision

Vision is the picture you have of profit in two to five years' time, and how you're going to achieve it

The Profitboss has a vision of success and he's determined to realize it.

It could be a vision of service excellence, of a new product range, of superbly harmonious employee relations, of exceptionally high-quality standards. In any event it will be a vision of how the profit is going to be achieved in the distant future.

To be meaningful the vision must be a detailed one, a vision of what will actually be happening in his area at 9.00 a.m. on Monday morning in two years' time to achieve success. It will be a vision of the minute-by-minute actions that are being taken by his team. It might be a vision of high-quality products being produced with minimal defects, or of consistently on-time deliveries with minimal customer complaints. It will, almost certainly, be a vision of 'trusting' employee relations managed by a team of Profitbosses.

It will be a vision of success from which everyone profits, a vision which the Profitboss has developed over many years, a vision in which he passionately believes and is able to communicate with enthusiasm to his team and every other employee in the organization.

His people will share the vision and strive for it too, creating their own personal vision of what is required, a personal vision which will mesh in with that of the Profitboss and the overall company.

TODAY'S STEP

Engage an independent consultant today (there are still one or two good ones left) and arrange to take your team away for a couple of days to brainstorm out a vision of success for the next two to five years.

Your objective must be to get your team totally committed to this vision (profit and all) and to a clear plan of action to realize the vision.

REMEMBER

The PROFITBOSS has a super-vision. He can see profit where others are at a loss to see anything.

Belief in product

Products need believing

If you believe cigarettes kill, you will never be able to sell cigarettes. If you believe your company manufactures the best food products, then you are more likely to do your best for the company.

Customers won't believe in your products unless you and your employees do. Customers buy product-belief: belief that your products are the best value for money, that they are the best quality, that they will receive the best after-sales service.

Product-belief has to be communicated. Ineffective advertising fails with disbelief. Superb advertising communicates a genuine belief that the product is unique and, what's more, superior to the competition. That belief has to be communicated within the company as well as outside.

The result is an accumulation of beliefs, from purchasing people who believe they have the best sourcing to manufacturing people who believe they have the most cost-effective production; from personnel people who believe they hire the best sales people to sales people who believe they sell the best products. The customers believe it too.

The Profitboss passionately believes in his company's products. He loves to go down to the factory floor and see the products being made. He loves to see the company's products being advertised, being stocked in the shops. He loves to see people buying the products and talking well of them too.

The Profitboss takes pride in his company's products and so does his team. They are all product-believers.

TODAY'S STEP

Inject some belief into your products and see the transformation into profit.

Determine today whether your people believe that your company's products are the best. If they don't, your top priority is to restore their belief.

If the quality of your products is poor, take action to improve it. Restore your people's belief.

If the design of your products is old-fashioned, take action to get it updated. Restore some belief.

Whatever your job, start developing some product-belief today!

REMEMBER

What the customer buys is a product of the PROFITBOSS's beliefs.

Risk-taking ability

The bigger the profit, the bigger the risk

The Profitboss takes risks every day. When he commits to a budget he takes a risk. When he initiates a new advertising campaign he takes a risk. When he hires a new sales person he takes a risk.

Every day the Profitboss is taking risks with people and company money. Every day the Profitboss is putting himself at risk.

Many managers attempt to escape the risk. With an extending family and a huge mortgage, why risk making difficult decisions and getting fired? Isn't it easier to pass the buck to your boss, some staff person or a committee? Then someone else can take the risk and carry the blame if things go wrong.

The Profitboss encourages risk-taking, knowing that in the absence of risk there will be an absence of decision and of profit. That puts the company at even greater risk. The Profitboss will risk people championing new ideas, and will support the idea with money, time and effort.

Risk is a matter of delegation, of trust, of knowing how to handle failure. The successful companies take risks because they have Profitbosses to whom they can delegate, whom they can trust to make 'risk-decisions' on their behalf.

Furthermore, successful companies know how to handle the occasional failure when the risk backfires. The last thing they do is fire the person who took the risk.

TODAY'S STEP

Be honest! When was the last time you took a risk at work?

Look back over the last week and count the number of 'risk-decisions' you or your team took.

If the answer is none, the company is at severe risk from your indecisiveness, your buck-passing. The comfort and security you are chasing can only be temporary with pusillanimous people like you prancing around.

Take a risk today. Get out and make some decisions which contribute to profit. Nobody's going to fire you for that!

REMEMBER

You have to risk everything to be a PROFITBOSS.

Professionalism

It is the amateurs who allow the professionals to profit

Making profit is a profession. It requires the highest ethical standards and immense skill.

There is only one qualification: money – The money you make and the way you make it.

The Profitboss received his professional training in the back streets of the business, selling ideas for peanuts and kicking garbage cans for profit. The Profitboss turns other people's losses into profit, and his competitors' profits into losses.

Street-wise and professional, his profession is to get the person on the street to know his product, buy his product and accept his product. His profession is to recruit the best person on the street to produce his product, to sell his product. His profession is to be streets ahead of the competition. His profession is to profit from the person in the street.

The Profitboss is a professional every minute of the day. Whether drinking coffee with his production people, chatting to his secretary or strolling along the corridor, his approach is professional. The same applies to answering the phone, writing a report or scheduling his diary. First and foremost, however, he is a professional leader, having devoted years of experiential study on how to lead teams of people to great success.

In every aspect of his job the Profitboss sets the highest professional standards. His professionalism is there for all to see, all the time. They see it in the high standards he and his people consistently achieve.

TODAY'S STEP

Don't be a Cinderella. Turn into a professional Profitboss today, whatever your job. Begin by setting exceptionally high standards in everything you do. For example:

- Think carefully before answering that memo. Being professional requires the highest standard of response – and that might not be another memo.
- Prepare very carefully for that meeting with the chief executive. Make sure that you have all the facts and can communicate the key points and recommendations succinctly and in a convincing way.

Having started on the road to becoming a professional Profitboss (whatever your job), now determine the other essential steps. It's up to you.

REMEMBER

To be professional:

- Don't waffle > Be honest
- Don't pretend > Be yourself
- Don't hide > Open up
- Don't duck and weave > Be straight and come clean
- Don't accept low standards > Go for the highest

FINALLY REMEMBER

The PROFITBOSS has only one profession.

Knowledge of facts

Business decisions based on opinion are in fact business decisions based on sand

Opinions are frequently worthless, while facts are of immense value.

The Profitboss carefully differentiates between fact and opinion, between fact and hearsay, between fact and guesswork, between fact and value judgement.

It is a fact that Joe has resigned, but not that Martha might. It is a fact that record results were produced last year, but not that this year will be even better. It is a fact that DLC suffered a pay strike last year, but not that they are against trade unions.

Large numbers of executives base their business decisions solely on opinions. They are ignorant. They pay scant attention to the facts, rarely being bothered to research them or substantiate them. What's worse, they often don't have the backbone to face the facts when these are presented to them. It's easier to find excuses for poor customer service than accept reality and do something about it. It's easier to dismiss reports of low employee morale than face the facts and act accordingly. It's easier to guess why a reduction in market share is taking place than obtain the basic facts and make improvements.

Facts convince while opinions provoke. Facts command authority while opinions undermine it. Facts speak for themselves, but only if executives are prepared to listen, are prepared to be convinced. The skill is in obtaining the facts and interpreting them. There can be no interpretations without facts.

The Profitboss knows how to get the facts, knows how to analyse, interpret and communicate them. He doesn't get immersed in detail but concentrates on the key factors having an impact on his profit.

The Profitboss profits from the facts, convincing his customers, suppliers, colleagues and team alike that he knows what he's talking about, that his conclusions and recommendations are based on solid evidence rather than unsubstantiated opinion. That's a fact!

TODAY'S STEP

Set yourself even higher standards of discipline in differentiating between facts, hearsay, opinions, guesses and qualifications.

Before you make any statement, either verbally or in writing, make sure you have the facts.

If you write, 'production has the worst absentee record', make sure you can substantiate it. If you say, 'Lewis doesn't communicate with his people', make sure you can substantiate it.

Discipline yourself to minimize opinion, disregard hearsay and reject guesswork. Furthermore, don't accept value judgements.

Discipline yourself to dig deep and get at facts which can be substantiated. It requires a persistent questioning approach.

Unsubstantiated half-truths and distortions of fact cause unnecessary argument and are an inefficient use of people's time. That's a fact! Or is it?

REMEMBER

The PROFITBOSS builds on the facts while tempering the opinions.

Decisiveness

Make profit by making decisions! The more you make, the better

Every decision at work has an impact on profit.

In a typical working day the Profitboss will make a thousand decisions.

He'll decide what hour he'll get to work. During the journey he'll decide on his priorities. He'll decide whom to talk to between the factory gate and the office. Later he'll decide what building and plant to look at.

The first thing he'll make on entering the office will be a profit-decision. It might just be to leave his door open. He'll decide to spend five minutes scanning his mail and raise key profit issues with Henry from Revenue Accounts, Glenda from Product Development and Bertie Buckles (his boss).

He'll decide to study the Pennington report and come to a decision on the recommendations. He'll decide to miss coffee and walk round 'A' plant. Then he'll decide to phone Carly Sheaffer at Sonarch on that supply problem.

Next he'll decide to go and look at how the new crimpling machine is working in the Wayfarer Bay. Finally he'll decide to go and tinker with his terminal to tell him the tally to date.

That's in the first hour. Then at 9.30 a.m., when his secretary brings in his mail, he'll decide how to spend the next hour and the rest of the day. Whatever his decision, it will be aimed at making profit. And at the end of the day he'll decide to assess that profit contribution.

Tomorrow there will be a thousand different decisions and even more profit.

TODAY'S STEP

Improve your decision discipline. Never pass up a decision, nor make a decision in automatic mode.

Bring into clear and detailed focus all the decisions you make today. Relate all your decisions to profit. If you can't, forget it. Don't waste your time on issues that bear no relation to profit. Just pass on to the next decision.

REMEMBER

1 The black and white decisions are easy.
2 Your skill will grow in making decisions in grey areas.
3 Better make a decision than none at all.
4 It's easier to get forgiveness for a poor decision than
   permission for a good one.
5 Making decisions means taking risks.
6 The more risks you take, the more profit you are likely to make!

FINALLY REMEMBER

There is only one criterion for the decisions a PROFITBOSS makes: will it make profit?

Uniqueness

It is commonplace to be second best, but to be best is to be unique

There is a sameness about many managers. Sucked into the bureaucracy of their organizations, they feel there are few opportunities for providing a unique contribution to profit, for distinguishing themselves with exceptional results. They lose their identity and become organization clones, never doing anything unique because they know that the organization would neither recognize nor appreciate it.

The Profitboss is preoccupied with uniqueness. To be successful his company must have a unique range of products and services which can be readily distinguished from the competition. It is that uniqueness with which people identify and which galvanizes executives and employees alike into positive high-performing action.

A Profitboss trains his people to understand the company's uniqueness; he talks to them about it. What's more, he makes sure that that uniqueness is sustained, that the competition never catches up. That means his people are unique too and have their own unique contribution to make to profit, whether they be in development, production, supply, marketing or administration.

Sexton, the security man at Gate 2, will perform effectively if he believes he has a unique contribution to make. The same applies to Penny the payroll lady. Their uniqueness must be linked to the company's uniqueness.

It is a key link for the Profitboss, a key factor in his unique leadership style, a key reason for his unique success.

TODAY'S STEP

Identify the areas of uniqueness across your company and also within your own areas of responsibility.

For example, spend five minutes over coffee trying to distinguish what is unique about your company's products and services.

What is unique about your own particular style of management? What is unique about the contribution you expect from each member of your team?

Identify your uniqueness today – and profit from it.

REMEMBER

The PROFITBOSS has his own unique way of making profit.

Openmindedness

Open up to the possibility of how closed your mind is

A closed mind is a small mind! A closed mind is when you believe that your way of making profit is superior to everyone else's. A closed mind is when you consistently believe that you're right and the other person is wrong. The Profitboss gets to the top because he believes that he could be wrong and could do better. He is always open to these possibilities.

Until the Profitboss makes a decision, he keeps an open mind as to what that decision might be. Before he resolves a problem, he keeps an open mind on how that problem might be resolved.

The Profitboss is reluctant to make judgements, knowing that his judgement could be wrong and the other person's right. He therefore only makes a judgement when a profit-decision has to be made, and in doing so takes the risk that he could be wrong. He is humble enough to admit the possibility.

To be openminded the Profitboss listens carefully, giving fair and genuine consideration to all ideas put to him. Listening is a difficult and complex skill at the best of times.

The Profitboss listens to Joe Cooper, the union representative, and his mind is open to the possibility that Joe could be right about certain aspects of the payment system being inequitable. The Profitboss's mind is open to the possibility that there might be too much bureaucracy in company secretariat when Paul the property services manager mentions it in passing. His mind is open to the possibility that Alan the Aston office manager might be pulling a fast one over him. His mind is open to the possibility that he might have made a mistake in hiring Stephanie to head Advertising and Promotions.

Overall the Profitboss is openminded to the possibility he could make even more profit. And as such he does.

TODAY'S STEP

Try to recall three ideas put to you by various people during the last week. Think through your reaction to these ideas. Did you automatically reject them? If so, why? Did you forget them? If so, why? Were you genuinely interested in these ideas? If so, how have you pursued them?

Open up your mind to the possibility that every suggestion someone makes to you is an opportunity for achieving even more profitable results.

REMEMBER

With his open mind the PROFITBOSS never shuts out profitable opportunities.

Courtesy

Courtesy is everything. It reveals the person

Courtesy is the mark of civilization. When the facades are swept away it is the use, misuse or disuse of courtesy that indicates whether a person respects you as a human being – or sees you and treats you as a nuisance, servant or enemy.

The values of respect, trust, dignity, equality, honesty, compassion, sensitivity, openness and sincerity are all reflected in the courtesies the Profitboss extends to people, whether they be customers, colleagues, acquaintances or members of his team.

Lack of courtesy is a disease in modern-day business. People don't reply to letters or return telephone calls. People arrive late or fail to turn up for meetings. People don't listen to others. People don't bother to say 'hello' or 'thank you'. People don't do as they say they will do. People make you feel small with a bored look.

Courtesy cannot be artificial. The programmed 'Have a nice day' lacks conviction, and courtesy means nothing without such conviction.

The Profitboss is sincerely courteous, taking a genuine interest in whoever he meets. He is respectful and values people for all the positive qualities they show, reflecting that value in the courtesies he extends to them. Thus the Profitboss is meticulous in replying to correspondence, whether it be a brief memo from a junior clerk in accounts or a personal letter from a salesman prospecting for business. He is meticulous in phoning back anyone who calls when he's out. He's meticulous in attending meetings on time. He's meticulous in saying 'thank you' for a good job done, or welcoming a visitor to his department.

Whatever the courtesy, the Profitboss is sincere about it. When he says, 'Enjoy your weekend' or 'Have a good trip' he actually means it.

TODAY'S STEP

Become totally conscious of the courtesies you use in your daily trans-actions with the people around you.

Spend five minutes appraising yourself (in other words, just think-ing – there is no need to write anything down) on this important issue, examining the detailed courtesies you regularly use.

Try to develop a discipline whereby you are consistently aware of and sensitive to other people and the courtesies that should be used to reveal this. In doing so make sure that you genuinely mean everything you say and do.

REMEMBER

The PROFITBOSS is meticulously and genuinely courteous in all his dealings with people.

Consistency

Consistency in management can only be fashioned from high principles

It's inconsistent decision-making by managers which precipitates organizations into confusion, disarray and low morale.

Inconsistency is when the personnel director, faced with a request for an increase in pay, says '4 per cent maximum' and then concedes 4½ per cent under threat of strike.

Inconsistency is when the wandering operations director says he'll look into the air-conditioning problem and then does nothing about it.

Inconsistency is when the top guy cries 'Communicate!' and then is too busy to do so himself.

Inconsistency is when directors use different toilets from the workers. What's different about their bodies?

People are rational, so rational in fact that they cannot understand the random nature of the decisions such senior executives make. These executives soon gain a reputation for being irrational and inconsistent, if not crazy. They lose credibility quickly with a resultant adverse impact on employee performance and profit. People feel threatened when decision-making is inconsistent and arbitrary.

The Profitboss is consistent. For example, he ensures that the investment in the new warehouse is matched by an investment in warehousemen. When the Profitboss requires 100 per cent punctuality, he means it. Nobody is late. That's consistency.

The Profitboss ensures that neither the aspiring Fenton from Fleet Sales nor the experienced Carmen from Marketing Services are denied the opportunity to compete for a promotion to Divisional Sales Director. That's consistency. It means 'saying what you mean and meaning what you say'.

The Profitboss initiates policies and practices that ensure all employees are consistently treated. He puts high value on consistent training, on consistent communications, on consistent remuneration schemes.

His consistency means that his people know what to expect of him, enabling them to work effectively within a clear framework of expectations.

As a key principle the Profitboss always manages for consistency. It is an essential key for achieving high levels of profit consistently.

TODAY'S STEP

Establish the underlying principles for every profit-making decision you take today. Application of the principle will secure a consistent approach.

Thus, if you have to choose between finding, in an already full diary, an extra half-hour to resolve an urgent customer problem or employee relations problem, establish the underlying principles: 'The customer pays our salaries and therefore must come first. But equal priority is my people. As a principle I will take one minute to communicate with my people, explaining why their urgent problem will have to be dealt with tomorrow.'

Be consistent in the application of your priorities. Be consistent in explaining to your people what's in your mind: they will understand, and understand you better, if you are consistent.

REMEMBER

The PROFITBOSS is so consistent you can read him like a book.

Service-orientation

Manage to serve, not to be served

The 'master-servant' class wars did nothing for the service concept, the implication being that he (or she) who serves is inferior. Inferior service resulted. In Britain particularly, people don't like serving and don't serve well. A smile rarely lights their face when they take your money and hand you the croissant. There is nothing inferior about a smile.

Western capitalism is based on service. That's the paradox.

He who buys is the 'master'. He who sells is the 'servant'. In an intensely competitive world it is the 'master-buyer' who has the power; the 'servant-seller' is weak and can only gain strength by providing a service superior to that of his competitors. Manufacturing the product is not enough. One has also to serve it well.

The Profitboss makes profit by 'out-serving' the competition. Better products, better prices, better quality, better delivery schedules, better maintenance standards, better customer relations and better service all round contribute to profitability. 'Giving the best' to the customer is an attitude of mind. It's called service-orientation.

Serving the customer involves more members of the company than just those who serve at the customer interface. Everyone in the organization serves: Accounts serve, Personnel serves, Manufacturing serves.

The Profitboss achieves high profits by getting everyone to serve together and serve each other. Communications serve well to achieve profit.

In too many organizations there is no concept of 'service-orientation'. People protect their own territories and are reluctant to put themselves out for other departments striving hard to provide a good service. The customer suffers as a result. Why wait in line at a bank, airport, hotel or shop? Why not go elsewhere where the service is better and someone will come forward from the back to help a hard-pressed colleague in the front line? Where the customer goes the money goes too.

The Profitboss goes where the customers are, and serves them well there and then.

TODAY'S STEP

Think of yourself as a 'servant'. Think of everyone you come across in your work as someone whom you are serving. It might be your boss, it might be the most junior person in your team. It might be the client at the end of the telephone.

Each time you make contact, identify the 'service objectives'. What are the other person's business needs and how can you best serve to meet them?

REMEMBER

There is no better servant than the PROFITBOSS.

Focus on end-results

Managers should be judged by their end-results

Whatever a Profitboss does, whatever a Profitboss thinks, he has only one thing in mind: the end-result.

The end-result of his meeting with Digby's Danny Davis. The end-result of a telephone call to Sandy Lil from Sanders. The end-result of a walk round the factory floor. The end-result of a letter to Chief Alhaji Hamman Maiduguri.

The end-result might be a second meeting, or some advice, feedback or a contract renewed. The end-result might just be to get a better understanding with his colleagues, or some improvement in team morale.

Every single action the Profitboss performs, every single decision he makes and everything he says are geared to an end-result.

The overall accumulation of end-results is his year-end contribution to profit: the achievement of budget, sales targets and effective employee relations. The year's end might seem a long way off but the minute-by-minute activities of a Profitboss are always directed to that end and the interim end-results required to achieve it.

Thinking constantly in terms of end-results maximizes the chance of achieving them. If you think only in terms of the problem of the moment and why it can't be solved, if you think only of what other people should be doing, if you think only of how you feel or what you want the other person to do, the chances are you will lose sight of the end-result and not actually achieve it.

One of the secrets of being a Profitboss is to identify and clarify the end-result of everything you do, everything you decide and everything you say.

TODAY'S STEP

Look at your diary for today and identify the end-result for every single meeting and action you have planned.

If you are to attend the monthly progress review meeting, think carefully about the end-result you wish to achieve by attending.

Try to relate the interim end-result of everything you do, decide or say to the overall profitable contribution expected of you at the year's end.

REMEMBER

Being a PROFITBOSS is an end-result in itself.

Conviction to the point of resignation

Always be prepared to resign

Organizations fail because managers compromise their principles. They put short-term expediency and selfish interest before the application of high principles.

The Profitboss will resign if he is instructed to recruit someone he doesn't believe can do the job. He will resign if he is forced to accept an unrealistic budget he cannot commit to.

The Profitboss will never commit unless he believes he can achieve. He'd rather resign.

Principles and beliefs are different from decisions and agreements. For instance, sometimes the Profitboss will disagree with a decision made by his boss; but that's rarely a reason to resign. Thus, while the Profitboss might think that the red logo has more impact, he'll accept his boss's decision to go for green. Opinion-based decisions are not issues of principle.

The Profitboss will accept decisions based on his boss's opinions. What he won't accept are decisions which compromise his principles: principles of openness, honesty and commitment amongst others.

TODAY'S STEP

As soon as you compromise your principles you are lost. Your people will stop believing in you. What's worse, you will stop believing in yourself.

Spend half an hour today working through in your own mind those issues on which you would resign (on principle).

Clarification of such issues and principles will give you immense strength in your management task – actually giving you more power to achieve your destined goal.

If there are no issues on which you are prepared to resign, think carefully. It can't be that you have no principles.

REMEMBER

On principle the PROFITBOSS will resign rather than profit without principles.

3
PROFITBOSS TECHNIQUES

Aiming to succeed
Entrepreneurial initiative
Determination
Being the best
Being in control
Managing time
Undertaking research
Attending to detail
Attaining quality
Helping others
Establishing the link to profit
Developing management
Taking criticism
Working from failure

Aiming to succeed

Success is relative. If you have never been successful, you never will be

Success is relative. Success is when you achieve your target 20 per cent return on assets at the year's end. Success is winning the Collesden Container contract against aggressive competition. Success is making the receptionist smile today and seeing her smile again tomorrow. Success is when you overcome Tuesday's supply problem with Maynard's.

Success is every positive contribution you make towards profit. Success is when you relax in an armchair on Friday evening, have a drink with your partner and forget about work for the weekend.

For the Profitboss every decision, every action, every piece of behaviour he and his team make have a criterion of success. They form the basis of an overall framework of success cumulatively indicated perhaps by the achievement of the annual sales, production or growth targets.

The Profitboss is only successful at the year-end because he strives to make every minute, hour and day of the week successful.

When he chats to Stuart from Corporate Planning, he strives for success. When he phones Tony the transport manager about delivery schedules, he strives for success. When he meets with the systems team to discuss the network, he is striving for success. When he walks down the corridor, he is striving for success.

The Profitboss doesn't assume that success will come at the year's end. He aims for success today and every day.

To that extent he doesn't think about problems, but only about this week's potential successes. He doesn't think about delays, only about on-time deliveries. He doesn't think about bad debt, only about positive cash-flow. He doesn't think about union problems, only about excellent employee relations.

He doesn't react to the negative but takes positive steps to be successful. The Profitboss believes that he can be successful. And he is.

TODAY'S STEP

Two tasks:

1 Review all your activities at work yesterday and appraise yourself. Were you successful in each?

　　When you talked to Tom from Internal Audit, was it a successful talk?

　　When you replied to that memo from Joan, the pensions manager, was it a successful response?

　　When you reviewed your business plan, did you conclude that to date you had been successful?

　　If you failed on one or two counts (and occasionally you will), what did you learn? How can you be successful next time?

2 Set yourself a standard for everything you do today and from tomorrow onwards. Every action you take, every word you say, every decision you make, every memo you write, every meeting you attend should be geared to success. You must identify the criterion of success for each. If you can't, forget it. Don't make the call, don't write the memo, don't attend the meeting. Instead devote your energies to something that will definitely be successful.

REMEMBER

The PROFITBOSS doesn't wait till the year-end to be successful. He is successful right now.

Entrepreneurial initiative

Entrepreneurial initiative is seeking out and seizing profitable opportunities

Everyone in the organization should be entrepreneurial – seizing initiatives to sell more, reduce costs, produce more efficiently and provide an even better service to the customer; seizing initiatives to secure new customers.

Everyone in the organization contributes to profit. There is no justification for paying a salary otherwise. Everyone in the organization can therefore seek out and seize initiatives to improve their contribution to profit.

The Profitboss develops an organization in which entrepreneurial spirit is encouraged not stifled, in which everyone can develop an 'entrepreneurial eye'. He encourages initiative, new ideas. He encourages risk-taking and tolerates the occasional consequential mistake.

In the Profitboss's team Hilda in Telephone Sales will not simply 'take orders' but will sell on to interested customers. That's entrepreneurial initiative. Jack, the boss at the Brighton branch, will not simply manage the supermarket but take entrepreneurial initiatives to advise customers of new product lines. Stella the personnel administrator will not simply push paper around in Personnel but will take action to cut down on the bureaucracy. That's entrepreneurial initiative. She'll just do it, not even asking permission.

The Profitboss himself will be keeping an entrepreneurial eye on the marketplace, seizing intiatives to improve services further and expand his customer base. It might start with a genuine smile, it might finish with a new 'high-class' service none of his competitors is providing.

TODAY'S STEP

Identify one entrepreneurial opportunity today, take the risk and seize it.

It might mean getting one additional customer in the shop or producing one extra unit in the factory.

It might mean selling one more inch of classified advertising space or encouraging one of your team to be as entrepreneurial as you.

The opportunity exists today. Be an entrepreneur and take it.

REMEMBER

There is no end to the entrepreneurial opportunities the PROFITBOSS will seek out and seize.

Determination

When you are determined to make profit, any problem can be overcome

There is no easy route to making profit. Obstacles, barriers, pitfalls and setbacks will always arise when you think you are getting there. Sometimes it seems you will never get there.

The Profitboss gets there – if not the first time, then the second time; if not the second time, then the thousandth time. His determination is underpinned by a belief that the problem, no matter how large it appears to be, can be overcome. It might be an apparently intractable problem with the union, with negative attitudes all round, with inequitable payment systems, with incompetent management and interfering personnel departments.

The Profitboss believes that the union problem can be overcome, that attitudes can be made positive, payment systems made equitable, management developed to be competent, personnel departments changed to be constructive. His determination is reflected in the actions he takes. He demonstrates his belief to the union that problems can be overcome, and if he fails to convince them the first time he'll try again and again. Ultimately he will convince them, his determination winning through, his belief becoming their belief.

The Profitboss will always find a way through to making profit. When others give up he'll still be running, convinced that the seemingly intractable problem can be overcome. That's determination, and that's the only way to make profit.

The Profitboss has the positive psychology of all successful people, a psychology which releases a surge of adrenalin whenever he experiences a setback or faces a seemingly insurmountable problem. It is a surge of adrenalin which makes him even more determined to achieve success.

The Profitboss never gives up. Only losers give up.

TODAY'S STEP

Show some determination today and start getting yourself out of the biggest rut you're in.

Identify the rut, and before you try to find the way out of it convince yourself you will get out of it.

Once you've convinced yourself you will get out of it, think positively and show some determination. Start the process of getting out. Your biggest rut can be your biggest challenge.

Determination, success and profit are all inter-related, they are all attitudes of one mind.

REMEMBER

The backbone of a PROFITBOSS is his determination.

Being the best

You can't really profit by being second best

There is never any merit in being second best. Whether you be a district sales executive, a vice-president finance or an operations manager, you must strive to be the best in your chosen area.

Being the best requires a special attitude. It means striving for excellence everywhere and every time, whether it be in the warehouse, reception, computer operations, the sales offices or elsewhere. It means superb performance day in and day out.

The people who make the biggest contribution to profit are those who take a pride in being the best. The Profitboss has the best recruitment and selection process. He has the best supervisor in his team and the best people throughout. He has the best training and development programme. Furthermore, he goes out of his way to ensure that his people get the best rewards for their labour.

Being the best means defining the best. The Profitboss devotes time and effort to this, taking his team away periodically to discuss their vision of excellence, clarifying it, refining it and defining it in terms of the best standards, the best contribution, the best performance. The standards might relate to punctuality, appearance or, for that matter, common courtesies. They will definitely relate to customer service and product quality. The contribution might relate to return on assets, employee productivity or product developments. The best performance might relate to daily production goals, sales targets or inventory levels.

Whatever the best is, the Profitboss communicates it to all the people in his organization, using keyline statements to get the message of 'the best' across in simple terms.

In a harshly competitive world the Profitboss knows that if he and his team are not the best, some other team will be. Losing to the competition is being second best. It's not an option.

TODAY'S STEP

Invest time in becoming the best and staying that way.

Plan to take your team away for half a day or a day. Hire a consultant to help. Thrash out with them what 'being the best' means for your department. Ensure that you gain their understanding and commitment to this vision of excellence.

'Being the best' doesn't mean having the best dreams. What it does mean is committing to actions to achieve the team's vision of excellence. Profit stems from the best actions, not the best intentions.

REMEMBER

The PROFITBOSS has no option: he just has to be the best in his chosen area.

Being in control

Bureaucratic organizations are those which get out of control with their controls

For the Profitboss his control is total. Yet it is hardly visible. He controls through the trust he develops in his team, his colleagues, his boss.

His control is hardly visible because he rarely attempts to control his team's methods of achieving their goals, trusting them to work within legal, financial and social constraints.

The Profitboss doesn't control his team's travel, nor their expenses, nor their recruitment, nor their international telephone calls, nor their use of agency staff or of consultants. The Profitboss doesn't control punctuality nor what his people say to the press.

His control is through their self-control. His control is through their commitment to forming a clear vision of success and turning it into reality, and that vision includes the highest standards of self-discipline.

Yet the Profitboss is not so naive as to believe that people do not occasionally betray trust, do not occasionally fiddle their expenses, do not occasionally get sloppy and hire unnecessary staff. He overcomes these problems not by imposing rigid bureaucratic controls which in themselves are expensive, but by developing his own sensitive antennae to detect people who step out of line.

He gets his deviants back into line with a firm, fair and consistent managerial approach.

Occasionally he'll ask a question such as: 'Why did you need so many taxis in Hong Kong?' It won't be a bureaucratic control, but it will be enough.

TODAY'S STEP

Don't waste your time setting up and maintaining expensive control procedures. Get rid of them today and develop some trust in your team.

Clarify your people's goals and get commitment to them.

For example, assign your service manager a budget and let him control his own expenditure.

For example, set your marketing manager the target of getting some positive publicity and let him control what he says to the press.

For example, set your production manager a quantified quality standard and let him control defects.

Be rigorous. Too many bureaucratic controls will lead to too little profit.

REMEMBER

The PROFITBOSS controls his own destiny, and his destiny is profit.

Managing time

Save time by finding time

There are always a thousand things to do. It is a paradox of modern-day business that, with time-saving devices such as desk-top computers, satellite telecommunications, electronic mail and supersonic aircraft, many managers find even less time to devote to essential profit-making activities – such as thinking and listening to people.

Time management techniques have become a fatuous fashion. Anodyne solutions are sought through an alchemy of systems that capitalize on consultants and capitulate on common sense.

The Profitboss's greatest skill is finding time: finding time for all those who would lose time without his help.

Paper is a waste of time, so he drops most of it in the waste bin. Committees are a waste of time, so he deletes them from the diary. Even darting off to foreign places can be a waste of time, so he delegates this to his deputies.

By dedicating at least five minutes a day to thinking through his use of time, the Profitboss manages to get his priorities right. His priority is people: it is through them that he makes profit. So he manages to dedicate an immense amount of time to people. In his view there is no other way to make profit.

Effective time management is based on clear thinking and common sense. You don't need a complex system for that – just time and some simple logic to begin with.

TODAY'S STEP

Find time to find time.

Don't overload your diary. Don't rush around. Don't find something to do just because you've got nothing to do. Don't feel guilty when you have a spare hour with no meetings, no mail and no interruptions.

Find time to think about the way you find time to think about making profit.

Find time to re-order the priorities in your diary. Discard all that time-consuming incoming rubbish and capitalize on your time for people.

Put people first in finding time for your pursuit of profit. It pays.

REMEMBER

The PROFITBOSS finds profit in the time he finds for people.

Undertaking research

The foundation of all profit is research

Being entrepreneurial is fine. Making decisions is great. Taking action is even better.

But it is not enough. Opportunities have to be researched. Decision options have to be researched. The appropriate action has to be researched.

Research will never eliminate risk, but it minimizes it. The less research you do, the more luck you need to make profit.

The Profitboss walks a tightrope between research and risk, between research and opportunity. Too little research and the risk will be too great. Too much research and the opportunity will disappear.

The skill of research is in accessing fundamental points quickly and substantiating them with hard data. Hard data is not precise data. Pursuing unnecessary degrees of precision (given the inevitable margin of error) is ineffective research.

The key to successful research is the ability to reject, at an early stage, fruitless lines of enquiry as well as trivia, opinions and unsubstantiated facts.

Research is the antithesis of randomness. Better a researched decision than a random one.

There is little random profit in this world. One has to research out the opportunities. That's how the Profitboss scores.

TODAY'S STEP

Don't leave research to the research department.

Examine carefully how you research your decisions. (Many managers can't be bothered to do any research and therefore make decisions they can hardly support.)

If you have to make a selection decision, for example, what information do you require and how do you research it? Are there better ways?

If you have to make a supply decision, how do you get at the necessary data? Are there better ways?

The secret of successful research is to identify clearly the 'profit' goal you are trying to achieve and then research all the options for achieving that goal as well as all the factors affecting its achievement.

Once you've thoroughly researched and analysed the facts, they should speak for themselves.

REMEMBER

The PROFITBOSS risks the research and researches the risk.

Attending to detail

Lack of attention to detail erodes customer confidence and profit

Customers aren't aware of your global strategy but they do notice little details like a badly typed letter, or a receptionist who's poorly dressed, or filthy ashtrays in the office, or torn packaging.

When you deliver at 3.00 p.m. on Friday, having promised Wednesday morning, the customer will take detailed notice. The same applies in the case of shoddy service, damaged products, faded displays and components that don't fit. The customer will notice all the detailed faults, taking for granted and not noticing the high standards of achievement in other areas of your business.

Detailed faults are incredibly complex to put right. They always erode profit. There should be no limit in the pursuit of perfection. Why should your customer accept imperfection?

The Profitboss doesn't manage the detail but only the people who get the details right. Through them he manages to achieve high standards of product, delivery and service. He manages to get every single person in his organization to pay attention to the smallest detail.

But he doesn't find it easy.

A traditional manager will attempt to do it by fault-finding and non-stop nagging. The Profitboss stresses the positive, emphasizing the importance of getting the details right for the customer. He counsels, he trains, he advises, always in a positive and constructive way.

He compliments his secretary on the perfect letter, reinforcing the positive. When she makes the occasional mistake, he points it out discreetly and quietly.

He compliments the production operator on the detailed attention he gives to the quality components coming off his line. When the quality occasionally drops, the Profitboss consults the same operator, seeking his advice on how to improve quality.

When there are detailed faults he never personalizes them. In that way he achieves the highest degree of attention to detail.

TODAY'S STEP

Put yourself in the shoes of your customers. Examine the detail.

You know how you feel when something goes wrong with something you've just bought.

How do you think your customers feel if their name is incorrectly spelt on a letter you send them, if the chrome is scratched on the door of the new car, if the pen doesn't work properly?

Do your company's vehicles look clean or dirty?

Do your staff always return telephone calls?

In your job there are a thousand details which you and your team need to pay attention to.

Get your team around the table and agree a plan of action to give even more attention to detail. You must get it right.

REMEMBER

By paying attention to detail the PROFITBOSS gets the pay-off in profit.

Attaining quality

Quality is an organization and management culture

You don't have to go far to see a lack of quality in the products and services many companies provide. The stained seats in an aeroplane, the cassette tape that jams, the hotel room service that arrives thirty minutes late, the bad apple in the pack.

It is easy to blame the machine, the computer or the system – but somewhere along the line a human being operated that machine, programmed that computer, used that system. Somewhere along the line a human being made a low-quality decision – and, what is worse, some supervisor or executive managed to allow it to happen.

The Profitboss does not run Quality Circles, but he does surround himself with circles of high-quality people capable of injecting quality into the products and services provided. It means that every decision or action taken between 9.38 a.m. and 9.39 a.m. on a Tuesday is high quality. And for every other minute of the working week too.

The desire for quality is an attitude of mind the Profitboss cultivates throughout the whole organization. He'll sacrifice nothing at the expense of quality, knowing that the customer will sacrifice him instantly if the quality of his goods or services is poor.

He'd prefer to see low profits today and high quality tomorrow rather than high profits today and low quality tomorrow. All his decisions are geared to investing in quality: quality people, quality training, quality machines, quality environment – all geared to quality products and services.

It's the high-quality Profitboss culture.

TODAY'S STEP

Do think quality every minute of the working day.

Do define quality standards and communicate these down the line.

Do check that these standards are being maintained. This means checking personally from time to time the output from your area, whether it be a shoelace, a bottle of beer, a written report, half an hour's advice or a telephone call to a client.

Do review quality with your people at least once a month.

Don't ignore quality defects. Take action immediately to rectify the problem at source.

Don't get defensive if anyone inside or outside the organization points to poor quality in your area. Be pro-active and do something about it **before** it is mentioned.

Don't ever forget about quality.

REMEMBER

The PROFITBOSS cultivates quality through his people.

Helping others

'I want to help you', if sincere, is ten times more profitable than 'Please help me'

Selfishness is a disease and is prevalent in industry today. It is self-interest based on a conviction that 'my needs are greater than yours'. It is reflected in attitudes such as 'I don't want to listen to you because I have more important things to say'; or 'I'm not interested in you because you can't help me'; or 'My way is always right, you have to understand'.

The Profitboss rarely seeks help, but he does go out of his way to provide it, even if he sees no profit in it immediately.

Not that he's a charity either.

He goes out of his way to help his customers, his suppliers, his employees, his colleagues and his acquaintances. While he knows he cannot directly relate all his 'help' to profit, he realizes that the creation of a 'helping' culture throughout his organization and beyond will yield dividends in the long term.

He's prepared to help whoever he meets, be it a trade union leader, a consultant or a junior clerk. Not that 'helping' means giving away money: giving help means giving time, thought and effort.

For the Profitboss help is not only an attitude of mind, but a way of life. He'll go out of his way to help Claudette the customer relations manager tackle a tricky complaint. He'll devote precious time to help Alan the auditor access the department's accounts. He'll take a positive interest in helping Ron Cally get a contract from Krite's.

In the end the Profitboss helps himself by helping others.

TODAY'S STEP

Establish a new discipline.

Whoever you meet, whoever you speak to, whoever you write to, ask yourself: 'Is there any way I can help this person?' If the answer is 'No', think again. If the answer is still 'No', think once again. Keep on thinking until you can discover ways of helping that person.

But don't impose your help on that person. Just communicate in a humble way that you are genuinely prepared to help. It's an attitude which wins friends and influences people.

As soon as you've learnt how to help people you will be surprised to learn how they can help you! And you won't even have to ask.

REMEMBER

The PROFITBOSS never refuses help to anyone.

Establishing the link to profit

**If you can't link it to profit, don't have it, don't do it:
it will contribute nothing**

Companies fail through their narrow view of what contributes to profit. They see only the direct links such as the number of sales people on the road, or the amount of raw material used. They fail to link, for example, working environment or management training to profit. These are the indirect links and they are as essential for profit contribution as the direct links. The problem is that they are harder to measure and therefore justify, and that's why hard-nosed finance people refuse to spend on environment and try to cut back training when it's the last thing they should do.

The Profitboss has a simple way of establishing the contribution link to profit. He asks himself two simple questions:

1 What is the specific contribution to profit of this resource or expenditure, or in making this decision, or taking this action?
2 Conversely, would there be an adverse impact on profit if this resource were removed, the expenditure not made, the action not taken?

Thus he'll ask:

- What contribution to profit does Judy make in her personnel job?
- What would happen to profit if Judy's job were eliminated?

- What contribution to profit would a refurbished reception facility make?
- What would happen to profit if the current dilapidated reception facility were retained?

- What contribution to profit would attendance at a 'leadership course' make for managers?
- What would happen to profit if the course were not run?

- What contribution to profit does this memo or telephone call make?
- What would happen to profit if the memo were not written, or the call not made?

Unless there's a positive answer, the Profitboss will take positive action to eliminate the non-contributing resource.

TODAY'S STEP

Go right through your organization and prepare a detailed resource inventory and expenditure schedule. Take each item and establish a contribution link to profit. To do so, eliminate each one (in your mind) from your operation. What would be the impact on profit?

If you don't know the answer you are managing ineffectively, squandering resources and making bad decisions.

Every paperclip, every business lunch, every job (and every item on the list) should have a contribution link to profit.

Remove the paperclips, remove the business lunches, remove the job, and if there's no adverse impact on profit, eliminate them.

Take action today to eliminate the resources and expenditure which have no contribution link to profit.

Be careful, though. Don't rush your decision. The vase of flowers in reception contributes more to profit than you think.

REMEMBER

The PROFITBOSS is the best contribution link to profit the company has.

Developing management

Management development should be an obsession

Most outstanding companies can be distinguished by one particular feature. They devote an inordinate amount of time, effort and resource to developing high-calibre managers. It is virtually an obsession.

Less successful companies at best 'dabble' in management development, occasionally sampling 'flavours of the month' or attempting 'magic wand' techniques for management training (acronymously labelled, for example, MIPS and PIPS). These companies pay lip-service to management development, fashioning their big progressive mouths with a cosmetic of highly developed lipstick techniques.

The Profitboss is obsessed with management development. He has working lunches with his team to discuss and develop their approach to managing people for profit. From time to time he takes his team away for a couple of days to provide a further stimulus. In seeking to develop managers he encourages each individual to develop a personal philosophy of management which can be implemented practically on a minute-by-minute basis each day of the working week. He spurns systems, gimmicks or fashion techniques peddled by consultants. He knows that individual managerial excellence can be achieved one day and lost the next.

To that extent the Profitboss sees management development as a permanent process, no matter how good the manager.

TODAY'S STEP

Management development starts with you. It's called self-development. Only you can make it happen.

Identify today and everyday some way of improving your effectiveness in managing people for profit.

For example, find out about the best workshops, seminars and training courses to attend. Attend them.

Talk to the management experts in your company (there must be one or two around). Learn from them.

Talk to your boss too. Learn from him as well.

The best way, however, is to benefit from your own experience. Sit down and jot down what you learnt yesterday. Self-confessed management mistakes should provide material for your own management development. (If you wait for the Personnel and Training Department to develop you, you'll wait forever. It's really up to you.)

REMEMBER

Developing a team of high-calibre managers is one of the
PROFITBOSS's highest priorities.

Taking criticism

The more criticism you accept, the more profit you will make

Self-righteousness in business is a sure way to lose money. It leads to automatic defensiveness, a syndrome by which the unions are always wrong, the customers – despite your attempts to appease them – are unreasonable and the people 'up there' don't understand.

Very few people know how to accept criticism. Yet criticism is the best source of learning. Criticism is constructive advice and should be nothing else.

When the staff at Bloomfield criticize the Profitboss for cancelling a visit three times running, he accepts it as constructive advice. He doesn't take it personally or make excuses when he gets his priorities wrong and other people point it out.

The Profitboss never lets his criticism become negative. Even when commenting on the poor service in the hotel he genuinely attempts to offer sound advice.

Acceptance of criticism leads to high standards, rejection of sub-standard performance.

Not all criticism, however, can be justified. When it's ill-conceived, ill-considered or based on incomplete information, the Profitboss won't criticize the critic. He'll just see it as another learning opportunity and advise accordingly.

The secret of criticism lies in the ability to depersonalize it. Criticism should never cause the recipient to lose face, inner dignity or self-respect.

Criticism should always be a positive move along the road to high profits.

TODAY'S STEP

You are not perfect. You know that.

Now is the day for self-criticism. Take yourself apart. Really have a go at it before someone else does. Criticize positively and constructively everything you're made of and everything you do (but don't destroy yourself in the process – you are no use to anyone as a nervous wreck with an inferiority complex).

Find at least three main areas of criticism of your performance on the job. Here are three examples to help:

- Do you get around enough to see your people – or do they criticize you for being too distant, frequently unavailable or too busy?

- Do your people really know what the team's profit mission is? Or do they criticize you for not really knowing where you're going? Or for being reactive and negative?

- Do you genuinely and sincerely investigate customer complaints and try to eradicate the causes? Or do you press 'button 39' and send out an automatic 'I'm sorry' response?

When you think criticism, think of yourself. Never go looking to criticize your team, your colleagues or your boss.

REMEMBER

In accepting criticism the PROFITBOSS suffers no loss of credibility.

Working from failure

Failure is the springboard for profit.

It is virtually impossible to succeed first time.

The Profitboss capitalizes on failure, does not let it destroy him. He learns from failure and gets his team to learn too.

Managing failure is one of the Profitboss's greatest strengths. It's the basis on which he develops his team. When Tim Franks fails to get the trucking contract with Tenby's, he helps Tim find out why. When Sheila Sheffield fails to achieve her quota for the quarter, he helps Sheila discover the reasons.

In life everyone fails more often than they succeed. Such is competition. The Profitboss succeeds because he is determined to turn failure into success. He knows that if he fails the first time, he'll win the second time, if not the third time. Even after ninety-nine failures he'll still be learning and still believe he can win. And he will, the hundredth time. There's enough evidence to show that perseverance pays off.

The real failures are those who give up and don't attempt to succeed at all after the first setback. If the Profitboss fails to please a customer today, he'll succeed in pleasing him or her tomorrow. If the Profitboss fails to deliver today, he'll succeed in delivering tomorrow.

Turning failure into success is an attitude of mind. It requires determination, perseverance and commitment.

Turning failure into success is what making profit is all about.

TODAY'S STEP

Admitting failure is the toughest test any executive can have. Any executive who fails to admit failure is doomed to fail anyway.

Be brave and list out your recent failures. (You cannot be that perfect!) Look critically at the root causes of those failures. (Why did you lose that contract? Why didn't you get that job?)

Don't blame 'the system' for *your* failure, blame yourself. Don't blame your boss for *your* failure, blame yourself. Don't blame the unions either, or the company, or Personnel, or Accounts.

It's best you blame yourself. Always try to make it *your* failure rather than theirs. That way you'll never stop learning.

Identify at least three key learning points stemming from your own personal failures and use these to learn to make even more profit.

REMEMBER

The PROFITBOSS doesn't plan for failure, but occasionally he fails with his plans. That's the starting point for his success.

4

THE PROFITBOSS
IN ACTION

Fight convention
Be pro-active
Negotiate with conviction
Audit yourself
Invest in new technology
Initiate new projects
Encourage protégés
Stop writing reports
Reduce inventory

Fight convention

There are no conventional ways of making profit

If everyone followed convention, no one would profit. Convention does not yield opportunity, does not prevent competition.

It might be convention to cut costs in times of crisis. The Profitboss might just go the other way and invest in revenue generation with a major advertising campaign.

It might be convention to lunch in the executive suite. The Profitboss will bring in sandwiches and a flask of tea, eating them with the fork-lift truck drivers in the despatch bay.

It might be convention to manage during the day. The Profitboss will come in at 2.00 a.m. and talk profit with the night shift.

He'll phone his customers with solutions before they phone with problems. He'll send personal hand-written letters when others send 'number 36' on the word processor.

The Profitboss is not a clone. He establishes identity through his unconventional approach. While the convention might be to undertake rigorous market analyses to identify new opportunities, the Profitboss is out on the street finding out what people want. While the convention might be to conduct attitude surveys, the Profitboss actually listens to his people.

Convention stifles creativity and initiative. The Profitboss encourages unconventional ways of making profit, encouraging his people to be creative and take initiative.

TODAY'S STEP

Shock everyone by doing something unconventional today.
  Here are some suggestions:

- Invite the most junior person in your department to sit in on your executive meeting.
- Convene an instant training workshop aimed at brainstorming out ten profit-making opportunities.
- Set your team a competition to increase profit levels by 10 per cent this week.
- Conceive a new product by the end of the day.
- Go home early.

REMEMBER

The PROFITBOSS sets the convention rather than following it.

Be pro-active

Pro-activeness is taking two steps forward while pushing your competition one step back

No one wins by defending. Pro-active attack is the winning way of the Profitboss. There is no profit in being re-active or retro-active.

Pro-active means giving your employees a pay rise before the unions demand it. It means offering existing customers the new model two weeks before they seek a replacement from your competitors. It means getting out on the road with the sales people before they complain about call schedules. It means getting down to 'D' plant half an hour before your boss rings your office to tell you to sort out the problem there.

The Profitboss has a nose for opportunities, for problems before they occur. He doesn't wait for things to happen, he actually makes them happen, initiating positive action, or stops them happening (preventing negative problems). That's being pro-active. He likes to be one step ahead of the pack, getting there before others do. That's the difference between leading and following.

When a customer sends in a rare letter of complaint, the Profitboss won't just send an apologetic, defensive, stereotyped letter back. He'll phone the customer, face the facts and pro-act his way to some repeat business.

Pro-activeness means putting your energies into moving forward to stay on top and keep the competition below. The opportunities are there every minute of the day and the Profitboss profits from pro-acting to them.

TODAY'S STEP

Pro-activeness is a state of mind. Try to identify what pro-active action you have taken over recent weeks. If you cannot do this, you are probably a negative reactor.

To become pro-active, keep an eye open permanently for opportunities to take further steps forward towards profit. Every piece of information coming into your office could present such an opportunity, so could everything anyone says to you.

Think laterally all the time and pro-actively seize the opportunities which other people will inevitably miss. Don't get sucked into the retrogressive reactive syndrome, responding only to problems after they have arisen.

Be pro-active now and prevent the problems arising tomorrow.

REMEMBER

The PROFITBOSS pro-acts his way to profit rather than reacting to potential loss.

Negotiate with conviction

Successful negotiating is all about the ability to say 'No' and mean it

Negotiating is a necessary evil. It is the antithesis of open, honest communication. It is the process of trying to persuade by substituting power for reason – the power being the ability to walk away from the deal and leave the other person stranded, the power to give the other person less than required – and sometimes nothing.

The Profitboss knows that he can only be successful in negotiations (whether they be with customers, suppliers or unions) if he is prepared to say 'No' when his 'prime' (price) objectives are not to be met.

The last thing he will do is reveal these 'price' objectives, never declaring his mandated 4 per cent maximum to the other side. Clarifying for himself the 'no' point or the 'sticking' threshold prior to the negotiation is a critical part of the Profitboss's strategy.

People fail in negotiations because they are frightened of the consequences of saying 'No'. So they give a little bit more, and more. They second-guess the other side's reaction, guessing wrong and giving too much.

The Profitboss is prepared to take the consequences of refusal. In fact he sees this as the key to negotiating success.

The key is to know where to draw the line and stop. The Profitboss therefore puts an immense amount of work into determining his final position prior to the negotiation. He ensures that this final position has the support of his boss and colleagues. Every negotiation needs that mandate. Too many negotiations fail because senior people undermine their negotiators by not backing a pre-determined final position.

The Profitboss will always negotiate from a position of power, yet try to persuade by reason, presenting the facts and figures of his case openly and honestly. He will not mislead with threats and bluffs. For him negotiating is less a game of poker and more a game of chess. Everything is above board except the strategy.

TODAY'S STEP

Prepare for your next negotiation by studying the lessons of past negotiations, the successes and failures.

Have you always been clear about your final position – have you always been prepared to stick to it, to take the consequences?

To what extent did you have the courage of your own convictions?

Negotiating is a test of courage, a test of your ability to say 'No' and mean it. Prepare to develop that courage, that ability today.

REMEMBER

The PROFITBOSS always backs his negotiators with the courage of his convictions.

Audit yourself

Trust yourself to be audited

The Profitboss never claims to be perfect. He likes to have the imperfections audited out of his system. So he does his own audit before the company audits him.

If he is accountable for production, he'll get his production operation audited: raw material wastage, machinery down-time, absentee levels, quality standards and many other factors.

If he is accountable for sales, he'll have his sales performance audited: call rates for the sales people on the road, repeat order levels, new sales, selling costs and expenditure on client entertainment. It won't stop there either.

If he is accountable for the warehouse, he'll have his warehouse audited: wastage rates, obsolete stock, retrieval rates, turn-over and wait-time at reception. There are other factors too.

He will audit his management team. Not that he doesn't trust them. But he'll want to audit their strengths, their weaknesses. Then he'll give feedback to eliminate the weaknesses and build on the strengths. He gets the audit done to help his team and they know it, welcoming it.

And he'll audit himself. Taking himself apart and putting all the bits (psyche and all) back together again. The Profitboss takes a broad and positive view about audit.

When he's carried out his own thorough audit, he'll be ready for the independent audit. And he'll have no problem with it.

For him a good audit is an asset.

TODAY'S STEP

Prepare an 'audit' action plan.

Look at all the critical areas under your control and devise an audit procedure for them. Don't rely on the company auditor: get yourself audited before he (or she) audits you.

For example, audit all areas of expense, all areas of material wastage, all stock levels. Audit your systems too, your people and your managers.

You don't need 'auditing systems' for this, just common sense.

Make sure, as part of TODAY'S STEP, that you explain to your people why you are carrying out this 'self-audit'.

REMEMBER

The PROFITBOSS audits himself before he audits others.

Invest in new technology

There are no old ways to make profit: new technology sees to that

New technology cannot be avoided. At best it is harnessed to make profit.

You will see new technology used by the best airlines, the best breweries, the best papermills and the best shops.

This might be obvious to you. It certainly is obvious to the Profitboss. But it's not obvious to the many who have failed to invest in the latest equipment, who continue to squeeze a poor profit from dilapidated plant, decaying property and – worst of all – disenchanted people.

Today it is virtually a sin to do without a computer in the office. Numeracy has a different meaning now. Yesterday you would just figure it out. Today all you have to figure out is how to let the new technology solve the problem for you. Tomorrow, unless you have new technology, you won't have time to figure out how to make the profit.

The Profitboss never says 'No' to new technology. It's like saying 'No' to profit. An investment in new technology is an investment in profit.

TODAY'S STEP

Answer these questions:

- Do you have a strategy for new technology?
- Do you even know what the latest technology is?
- Do you know the cost of investing in new technology?

Ring round the experts and take some advice today. Then get a terminal on your desk and capitalize on the investment immediately.

REMEMBER

There's new technology in the brain of a PROFITBOSS.

Initiate new projects

Project yourself out of the routine and into profit

There is no routine way to make profit. It is dangerous therefore to allow people to think they have routine jobs. Change is essential. Projects are essential.

What's more, routine jobs bore people. Projects stimulate them.

The Profitboss is a project manager. In his team Rachael Ross spearheads a project to improve telephone sales, John Little leads a project to reduce wait-time at reception, Bob Reynolds is completing a project on extended opening hours and Edna Kelly is initiating a project to eliminate unnecessary bureaucracy. There's profit in all these projects. And all these projects are additional to the normal jobs of the people in charge of them.

Projects allow people to broaden their career horizons, to gain new experiences. Projects have a start-point and finish-point, and the finish always provides enormous satisfaction. (Routines never satisfy.)

Projects are akin to change. Putting people on projects is a positive way of making them change-agents, of putting into practice all those fine theories about involvement and participation.

Projects should stretch people, not overload them; projects should provide excitement on the job, not stress and strain.

The Profitboss uses projects as a positive motivational force, not as a method of exploiting his team's goodwill.

TODAY'S STEP

Review the projects you and your team have under your wing at the moment. Are they providing a positive motivational force?

Are they likely to contribute to profit in the long term?

Devising and working on projects is one of the most creative ways of managing people for profit.

If, as a manager, you have no projects, look at all the 'change-opportunity areas' under your control. Your department cannot be that perfect. Establish some short-term projects to make improvements and get your people involved.

Project them into profitable change.

REMEMBER

The PROFITBOSS project-manages his profit year by year.

Encourage protégés

Tomorrow's profit comes from today's protégés

Ordinary people produce limited profit, sometimes none. A talented competitor will always beat them.

The Profitboss earmarks talent. He is not ashamed of developing a small group of talented protégés who will spearhead the attack on the competition. They prove themselves by becoming élite performers who climb rapidly through the organization.

He chooses these people carefully and objectively, always with an eye on potential success. He'll devote time to them, teaching them, encouraging them, supporting them, providing them with opportunities to develop their unique talents.

He'll defend to the hilt charges of 'favouritism', 'the blue-eyed boy syndrome', 'the chosen few'. When you are shooting for high profits, you have to have a small entrepreneurial team who can project their way forward, not today but tomorrow. That's why the Profitboss has his protégés. He's thinking of tomorrow's profit.

Investing time in identifying and developing 'profit protégés' is a priority for the Profitboss. Not that he will ignore the larger majority of his people who form the reliable, hard-working backbone of his organization: he'll devote time to them too, perhaps explaining his policy and practice for developing flair in his team.

TODAY'S STEP

Who are your protégés?

Who are those talented young people rising fast through your organization?

Who are the people who will be annihilating the competition tomorrow, securing even higher returns for the company?

Identify them today. Don't wait for Personnel to come along and do it for you.

Then decide how you're going to develop these people. Invest time, this week, next week and every week in encouraging and supporting this élite team, making sure that you provide them with development opportunities.

If you can't do all this, the probability is that you don't have any talented people around (in which case there's no way you'll be successful and profitable tomorrow). Change tack immediately and take urgent action to get some talented protégés into your fast lane.

REMEMBER

In choosing protégés the PROFITBOSS is interested only in performance and potential, not patronage and politics.

Stop writing reports

A thirty-second verbal report is thirty times more valuable than a thirty-page written report

Writing reports can become an addiction. At its extreme everyone ends up spending all their time writing reports on everything they do.

Sales people complain most of being burdened with the problem, having to spend valuable days in the office (when they could be out selling) writing reports to head office about customer contact, new leads and lost sales.

Personnel people are the worst afflicted with the ailment. They write reports on everything, from leaking toilets to confidential leaks.

The problem is not only having to write the report but burdening countless other people with the chore of reading the bloody thing. There are managers who are not highly literate in any case and who don't know how to put a report together. Because their reading skills are poor too, many reports end up in the waste bin – which is a better place for them than the filing cabinet.

The Profitboss goes out of his way to discourage report-writing: to do so he will go out of his way to walk the patch and give (or obtain) thirty-second verbal reports.

Verbal reports always precede written reports in any case (on the grapevine), thus making written reports redundant along with the managers and secretaries who waste precious time writing them.

There is a case for writing reports but the Profitboss prefers not to make it, preferring to profit from an accurate word of mouth. He finds it much more effective to keep his distance from the in-tray.

TODAY'S STEP

Stop writing reports. Stop reading reports.

Free all that valuable time wasted on such bureaucratic chores to go and listen to a few people who have something important to say.

REMEMBER

Reporting to the PROFITBOSS is not a paper exercise.

Reduce inventory

If it won't earn you profit within the next three months, cut it from your inventory

It shouldn't be there if you don't need to use it. If you need it in three months' time, buy it in three months' time.

The worst thing you can do is buy things you will rarely, if ever, need. Most managers do. They allow their secretaries to hoard three years' supply of sticky tape, their personnel people to stock six years' supply of appraisal forms (when most managers would do better with blank sheets) and their engineers to 'buffer out' with an indefinite supply of obsolete parts.

These stockpiles of sanitized 'rainy day' rubbish can make the difference between a miserable bottom-line result and a sparkling performance.

The Profitboss is rigorous about inventory. He gets it checked as frequently as he checks the bottom line. He is intolerant of fat and ruthlessly disperses it. He is meticulous in developing, implementing and maintaining systems which minimize inventory and maximize profit.

One spare nut on a table may not seem much of an asset, but 10,000 nuts going spare are a liability.

The Profitboss screws down his inventory before he screws up his profits.

TODAY'S STEP

Take a pencil and pad and estimate the cost of all the rubbish in your office.

If you're never going to read those twenty-year-old management books collecting dust on your office shelf, make some profit (it's always best to start in a small way) by selling them to a secondhand bookshop. The space you release can be used most profitably.

Now repeat the exercise around your department. Question people about those unused cans of oil, those untouched containers full of rusty rivets, those unopened boxes of insulating foam. Get rid of the surplus!

Take it further and closely examine the warehouse. Look carefully at the inventory control system. Does it tell you what you want to know? If not, change the system. You must get to know your inventory if you know you're going to achieve profit.

REMEMBER

The PROFITBOSS tests the efficiency of his team through their inventory control.

5

PROFITBOSS PSYCHOLOGY

Personalizing the organization
Creating identity
Studying psychology
Being a diplomat
Sharing confidences

Personalizing the organization

An organization is bigger than the sum total of its people. The difference is profit

Organizations can appear sinister. Somewhere up in the clouds there is a faceless organization man who menaces people with punitive restrictions, stifling rule-books, unyielding systems and incomprehensible decisions.

This anonymous 'Big Brother' dominates people's lives, sometimes threatening to destroy them. The branches of the hierarchical tree hide this secret organization with its inner clan of unknown lieutenants possessing mythical powers. Down at the grass roots, deep fears are generated about what's happening 'up there' in the organization: deep fears about promotion, pay, performance and job security. The organization becomes a drag-net for the worst excesses of commercial endeavour.

The Profitboss steps in to defuse any fears about the organization, generating first and foremost a belief in himself: a belief that he will fight for his people in the pursuit of profit, a belief that he will reciprocate their care and concern for the organization, a belief that he will be trustworthy in his communications.

For the Profitboss an organization is a team, not a meance; a team in which the key players are known and respected. He develops the organization by developing the team, clarifying accountabilities and showing genuine appreciation, consistently, for each individual's contribution to profit.

By developing an organization with clear accountabilities, he can provide clear explanations to his people about decisions made from 'on high'. He knows who to go to for explanations. Openness and honesty involves the application of clear accountability and is the hallmark of any successful organization. An erosion of that openness and honesty, a muddling of those accountabilities and a restriction on clear communication will lead to demoralizing fears about those sinister elements 'up there' in the organization.

TODAY'S STEP

Clarify the organization today.

When your people talk about 'the company' (the organization), whom are they talking about? Make sure they know.

For example, when they say: 'The company should spend more on training' or 'The company should do something about its advertising,' what do they mean by 'the company'? To whom in the company are they referring? Who are these anonymous people in the organization making decisions on pay ('The company should pay us more') or on other issues ('The company should take a tougher line against the competition')?

The answer should be simple. You are the boss. You are the company. You are the organization. And that applies whether you be a supervisor or a senior executive.

When your people talk about the organization, they should be talking about you. Make sure they do, starting today. You represent the organization in their eyes. It should be no other way (there is no other way). If you don't like bearing the weight of the organization on your shoulders, you should resign. Don't be a small child with a big brother of an organization. Get out and speak for the organization today, and be honest. It's the most profitable thing you can do.

REMEMBER

The PROFITBOSS is the organization.

Creating identity

Giving identity to profit contribution is an essential executive task

If you identify with the profit-goals of the company, it is essential that you identify every single contribution to profit.

The Profitboss identifies his southern sales team as the most successful in the organization. He proclaims their achievements in front of all. He gives them identity.

The Profitboss encourages his people to identify with the company's new '2000' range of products, to identify their own contribution to its potential success in the marketplace.

The Profitboss identifies Marilyn McGregor as the top-ranking customer service engineer, highlighting the stream of compliments she gets from the field.

By giving identity the Profitboss helps develop a sense of pride in the company's profit achievements. By giving identity the Profitboss recognizes and appreciates each individual's contribution to profit. By giving identity the Profitboss creates his own identity as a leader with a clear profit-mission who has the total support of his team.

People need identity. A name is not enough. The company, the product, the team, the achievement, the location and the job all contribute to identity.

The Profitboss creates that identity, an identity for each individual in the team as well as for the team itself. He does it by bringing into focus the various contributing factors. In that way he ensures a total identity with profit.

That's why people identify with a Profitboss.

TODAY'S STEP

Identify the contribution to profit you have made in the last four weeks.

If you cannot do this, the company is wasting its money on you.

In identifying this contribution, make sure you are 100 per cent clear about how each single decision and action you took related to profit.

Now carry out a similar process for every member of your team. If you identify an outstanding contribution to profit, proclaim it at your next team meeting. Give identity to the achievement.

REMEMBER

Achieving profit is the only thing that gives identity to a
PROFITBOSS.

Studying psychology

Psychology is the key to making profit through people

Customer psychology, leadership psychology, management psychology, occupational psychology, organization psychology, employee psychology, trade union psychology and personal psychology: the Profitboss has made a life-long study of them all. He is an expert in psychology.

To make profit you don't have to understand complicated profit-and-loss accounts. What you do have to understand is what motivates a customer to buy a small green apple as opposed to a large red one.

You have to understand why Larry Parks runs five miles to work, why Fiona Isaacs is always smiling and Barry Greystone is always failing.

To profit through managing people successfully you don't have to understand discounted cash flow, exchange provision, accrual and depreciation. You can leave that to the experts, the accountants. But you do have to understand accountant psychology.

The Profitboss studies psychology every minute of the day. It is a simple matter of studying people's minds, observing their behaviour and analysing their attitudes.

It is a simple matter of relating their minds to profit: customer minds, colleagues' minds, suppliers' minds, employees' minds and your own mind.

TODAY'S STEP

Observe behaviour. Analyse attitudes.

What was really in Chris Christiansen's mind when he knocked on your door? How did the issue he raised relate to profit?

What was really in Judy Jackson's mind when she lost her temper? How did the issue relate to profit?

What was really in your mind when you went to talk to Gene Holly? How did it relate to profit?

Behaviour is deceptive, frequently misleading. To understand it you have to be a psychologist.

Try to understand the basic motivations of the people with whom you are working. Try to understand their excitements, their joys, their satisfactions, as well as their fears, their concerns and their doubts. Try to differentiate between heart and mind, between behaviour and attitude, between thoughts and emotions.

Try to understand what's in people's minds; because when you understand that much better, you'll have that much better a chance of making profit.

REMEMBER

The psychologist in the PROFITBOSS sees the profit in you.

Being a diplomat

Diplomacy is making a loser genuinely feel like a winner

Diplomacy is a delicate balance of integrity, honest communication and maintenance of face.

In the commercial world diplomacy is profiting through people, not from people. It is turning unpalatable decisions into palatable ones. It is making the poor feel rich. It is getting people to accept painful decisions without hurting them.

The biggest danger in diplomacy is falseness, dishonesty and lack of credibility. Diplomats can live on a brilliant surface of respectability and still risk sliding into the mire of distrust hidden below.

When you have to take money out of other people's pockets (which is what profit-making is all about) you can do it either by inadvertently alienating people or by deliberately getting them on your side. The Profitboss always does the latter. He is a diplomat.

He displays a wide range of diplomatic skills such as always speaking the other person's language, being acutely sensitive to customer needs and creatively expressing genuine appreciation for a job well done.

He is always positive and courteous at the same time as being astute, determined and unwavering in his pursuit of profit.

The key to diplomacy, however, is inner dignity. The Profitboss goes out of his way to preserve 'face'. No matter how humble the person with whom he is dealing, he always respects that person for his or her positive qualities.

TODAY'S STEP

Invite the person closest to you to give you some honest feedback on the degree of diplomacy you exhibit.

If he (or she) is really honest with you, you might be surprised at the level of rudeness, insensitivity, indifference and selfishness you occasionally show. (Even if you see it in other people, you might well not see it in yourself.)

Start a simple course in diplomacy today. Make sure you say 'Thank you' for a job well done.

Take an advanced lesson tomorrow and call up the poorest performer in your team (there must be one) and make him or her feel really good about the challenge ahead. That will be profitable. It will also be diplomatic.

REMEMBER

There are two ways to make profit, the barbaric way and the diplomatic way. The PROFITBOSS always chooses the latter.

Sharing confidences

Never profit from a confidence, but make profit in confidence

Sharing confidences is essentially a two-way process. It is unrealistic to assume that a junior will confide in you unless you are prepared to confide in him or her. Conversely, it is unrealistic to give a confidence unless the other person is prepared to reciprocate in confidence.

Grapevine gossips, leakages of confidential information and other communication abuses often result from senior executives totally mis-understanding the vital management task of sharing confidences.

In an aggressively commercial world where competitive information is carefully guarded, and in a humanitarian world where personal rights are painstakingly protected, the handling of confidences and confidential information becomes a highly sensitive and valuable management skill.

To achieve the highest levels of profit the Profitboss sets to achieve the highest levels of trust within his team.

Trust has to be demonstrated. The Profitboss demonstrates it by taking his team totally into his confidence. He never allows them to be shocked by finding out things before he tells them. They are the first to be advised of impending re-organizations, of imminent appointments, of new market-ing initiatives and planned strategic changes in direction.

In turn, the Profitboss knows that he will be the first to be advised of personal issues troubling his team. Unless confidences are shared within a trusting team, problems often fester and subsequently explode. There's no profit in that. It's far better to defuse the problem at the start.

In encouraging the sharing of confidences the Profitboss takes care to ensure that the confidence is not abused, taking to task any team-member who betrays the trust.

TODAY'S STEP

Do you take all your team into your confidence?

Conversely, do they trust you sufficiently to discuss with you those delicate and sensitive issues which need confidential handling?

If the answer is 'no' to both questions, you have serious problems in your team which will inhibit your profit performance.

Starting today, examine ways of developing trust within your team. Give a confidence or two and see how positively they react. Encourage them to bring forward issues of concern and listen carefully. Treat as completely confidential any information they bring to you.

REMEMBER

The PROFITBOSS totally trusts every member of the team and shares every confidence with them.

6

THE PEOPLE IN THE LIFE OF A PROFITBOSS

Achievers
Colleagues
Secretaries
Subordinates
Finance people
Administrators
Consultants
Experts
Union representatives

Achievers

Achievers turn their jobs into profit-making opportunities

The Profitboss surrounds himself with achievers: Frankie Dockertz who achieves the most efficient warehouse operation in the region, Liz Mills who has eyes for selecting the best sales people in the country, Betty Boyd who provides the most reliable administrative back-up in the company. And there are others, too – like Sue Galloway, perhaps the friendliest receptionist anywhere. The customers love her.

They are all achievers in their own right and the Profitboss knows it and appreciates it. His achievement has been to turn their jobs into achievement opportunities for making profit. Sue sees the profit in a customer's smile. Betty sees the profit in achieving a twenty-four-hour response time on all customer enquiries. Liz sees the profit in investing two days' selection time to hire a top-flight sales person. Frankie sees the profit in getting a one-hour turn-around on the trucking operation at the warehouse.

When the Profitboss takes coffee with Wally Brown, the fork-lift driver, he'll ask him straight: 'Wally, what did you achieve yesterday?' Wally will know, because the Profitboss would never have let him keep his job if he didn't.

In an intensely competitive world, if any team-member doesn't know what contribution to profit he or she should make, the probability is that profit will not be achieved.

TODAY'S STEP

Look at each member of your team. Are they achievers? What did they achieve last week?

If you don't know, the probability is that they don't know either (and someone will catch up on your lack of achievement later).

Starting today, identify your team's achievements and turn each member into an achiever.

It's the only way to profit.

REMEMBER

To profit, the PROFITBOSS cannot make it all himself. He must have achievers in his team.

Colleagues

Your colleagues should profit from having you around

Never take profit from your colleagues. Never fight them or exploit them. Don't run them down with bitchy comments behind their backs. Don't play politics. Your colleagues are there for the same reason as you, no matter what they might say or do.

Let them profit from your membership of the team.

The Profitboss places few demands on his colleagues, nor does he expect favours. The last thing he'll do is attempt to show them up.

The first thing he'll do is help them. Whatever the occasion, whether it be over coffee or in a contentious meeting, the Profitboss goes out of his way to assist his colleagues. He finds time for them, always being prepared to lend a sympathetic ear or give some friendly confidential advice.

The Profitboss values the team he works with, values the contribution each member makes to profit. He'll never get in the way of this, never complaining that 'things are too difficult', never creating barriers in the way of helping them.

He knows that if he helps them in time of need, they will reciprocate without being asked.

No matter how difficult some of his colleagues might be, no matter how incompetent, negative, bad-tempered and unco-operative they are, he will always persist in trying to develop constructive meaningful and friendly relations with them. The last thing he'll do is relapse into back-biting politics and team warfare.

If he has anything to say about them, it will be constructive and helpful. And he will say it in front of them.

Everyone should profit from having a Profitboss around.

TODAY'S STEP

Put yourself in the shoes of your colleagues. Go out for a walk with them and forget your problems: just think about theirs. What is more important – that they achieve their goals or you yours? The answer must be the former. So today identify two ways in which you can help your colleagues achieve their goals.

It might just be the voice of support at a meeting or the follow-up on a personal problem mentioned a few days ago.

But first of all you have to walk in their shoes and understand their problems. That requires time. So give your colleagues some today.

REMEMBER

In pushing for profit the PROFITBOSS pushes for his colleagues.

Secretaries

A manager is as good as his or her secretary

Secretaries are difficult, mainly because they try to manage their bosses. Other members of the company will be aware of this, and it reflects on the credibility of the boss.

The Profitboss lets his secretary do her job, not his own, carefully differentiating between the two. He is sensitive to her situation, never interfering or interrupting when she's under the pressure he's already created for her.

The Profitboss takes his secretary into his confidence, seeks her opinion, takes her advice. He ensures that she (if it is 'she') works to his high standards and, furthermore, has the social skills to handle all types of people. He finds time to talk to her and tell her what's going on so that she's never at a loss to deal with any situation.

While lesser managers permit their secretaries to gossip, back-bite, return late from lunch and produce sloppy memos, the Profitboss knows how to get the best out of his secretary. He appreciates her, recognizing her good work, thanking her when she works late. He'll buy her a small gift when she's made an exceptional contribution.

Occasionally he'll take her out to lunch. But you'll never see the Profitboss sipping late-night liqueurs with his secretary. He knows where to draw the line and so does she.

TODAY'S STEP

Chat to your secretary for half an hour. Take an interest in her work and find out how she feels about the way things are going. Seek her advice on what is happening in your department.

Give your secretary some time today and then she'll do her best for you.

Come Friday, take her out to lunch (and make sure that it's the best restaurant around and, furthermore, that you pay – not the company).

REMEMBER

A super-secretary is an extension of the PROFITBOSS.

Subordinates

The most agreeable way to manage is to subordinate yourself to nobody

Subordination is a Victorian concept and should be defunct. It is incompatible with equality.

Everyone in an organization should have a clearly defined role. Ideally a manager's role is to make profit-making decisions which enjoy the consensus of the people around him. There is no requirement for subordination within this ideal.

In practice decisions have to be made with which people disagree. Acceptance of decisions with which you disagree is not akin to subordination. In a team where mutual respect exists, the leader will be trusted to make the best decisions, even if they go against your views.

To be subordinate is to accept without challenge the ascribed authority of another.

The Profitboss requires no such authority. He facilitates his people's work rather than authorizes it. To that extent he is subordinate to them, carrying out an 'enabling' role.

Authorizing expenses, travel and recruitment are forms of bureaucratic control rather than manifestations of subordination. Where it counts – achieving spectacular results – everyone works as a team. And that team is led by a Profitboss. He doesn't consider his team-members as subordinates, always consulting them, always seeking consensus, always doing his best for them in the decisions he makes. That's not traditional subordination.

Traditional subordination is arbitrary, exploitative and alien to the modern values of management by commitment.

Pete the packer, Dickie the driver and Chloe the cleaner all accept that the Profitboss has greater skills in prioritizing their work than them. They respect his unique role. Conversely, the Profitboss accepts that they have greater skills in packing, driving and cleaning than him. He respects their roles. It's called mutual respect and it's the opposite of subordination.

TODAY'S STEP

Eliminate the word 'subordinate' from your vocabulary.

Eliminate any thoughts that you have power over the people in your team.

Treat everyone as equals, none as inferior.

REMEMBER

If anything, the PROFITBOSS subordinates himself to his people.

Finance people

The best finance people don't value the business just in terms of money

The trouble with most finance people is that they see things only in terms of money. It is a limited view. Their narrow perspective alienates them from broad-minded people who value the business in broader terms, who value certain immeasurable but critical factors such as morale, expertise and goodwill. What price a positive attitude?

The Profitboss knows the value of an excellent working environment and will fight hard against the narrow-minded finance people who demand a detailed profit justification for investing half a million in improved conditions. What cost de-motivation?

The Profitboss knows the value of excellent customer relations and will resist any attempted reduction of travelling and entertainment expenses by short-sighted finance people. How do you measure goodwill?

The Profitboss knows the value of a good pay increase and will rebel against the mean-minded finance people who try to screw employees with bare minimum wages. (The Profitboss is ten times more effective than a union.)

Finance people are simple-minded. They have uni-dimensional minds, thinking only in monetary figures and knowing only how to subtract costs from revenue. They value everything they can get their hands on. But they can't value employee attitudes, or working environment, or training or any other indirect variables with unquantifiable benefits.

The Profitboss is wary of finance people, seeking their support but running miles to avoid their control. He commits to a budget and achieves it. Never will he let a finance executive (or even his boss under the influence of one) impose a budget on him.

Having committed to a budget, never will he let the finance people tell him how to get there. He knows he can't win the race with his hands tied behind his back, or his toes chopped off.

The best finance people are more of a help than a hindrance. That's the type of finance people the Profitboss invests in.

TODAY'S STEP

Honestly evaluate your relationship with the finance people around you.

Ask yourself these questions: How much influence do finance people have over the achievement of your goals? Do they effectively manage your empire with detailed rules on expenditure? Do you have as much influence as them? Do they control you? If so, what do you control? Do you manage to protect critical but unquantifiable benefit areas such as training, environment, product quality and customer service?

Are the finance people running your life for you? If so, it's about time you rediscovered your powers of persuasion.

Aim to persuade them today of the value of investing in immeasurable things. Make sure you win. Just tell them how you're going to make all that additional profit. They must agree (unless they're idiots!).

REMEMBER

The PROFITBOSS takes advice from finance people, but never decisions.

Administrators

Managers should *never* be administrators

Over the last few decades the distinction between leaders, managers and administrators has become increasingly blurred, to the detriment of profit and people alike.

Many a manager has ceased to be a leader and has been sucked into the bureaucracy of his organization, effectively (in many cases ineffectively) becoming just an administrator of the cumbersome systems within it.

Leadership is all about securing the high performance of a team to achieve a specified goal. Many managers interpret that as being an administrative chore, filling in objective work-sheets and completing performance appraisal forms.

The Profitboss is not an administrator. While he believes in and requires effective administration, he leaves it to the experts, to the people who have a flair for making things happen through systems and computers, and paperwork. That's administration.

Administration is despatching Gary Gibson and his gang of three to the Golden Gables site while Tim O'Reilly's team go to the Trinidad Complex. Administration is ensuring that Gary and Tim get back-up supplies, are advised of scheduling changes and get paid on time.

The Profitboss delegates all that. He sees his job as motivating Gary Gibson and Tim O'Reilly to achieve the highest profitable performance at Golden Gables and Trinidad. The last thing the Profitboss will do is stay in the office to administer the paperwork on these projects. His administrator will do all that. He'll be out and about, communicating with the likes of Gary and Tim to ensure that they understand how profitable their contributions are.

TODAY'S STEP

Carefully examine your work-load and identify and question all elements of administration.

Don't automatically accept that it's all necessary. Challenge everything. Can you eliminate some of the administration – or pass it on to the administrators – thereby releasing your time for more profitable activities?

For example, question whether you really need to see all those monthly reports crammed full of data you never study. Do you really need to get involved in the administration of payroll changes, budget procedures, cheque authorizations and production schedules? Far better leave this to the experts.

Cut out some administration today and put more time into leading your people to an even more profitable contribution.

REMEMBER

The PROFITBOSS takes the paper out of management and gives it to the administrators.

Consultants

The best consultants are as hard to find as the best managers

Ninety-five per cent of consultants are drop-outs. The rest are stars. In fact, they are light years ahead. They have made it and can help you make it. That's their mission. The best are the one-man bands who excel at all the things the large corporate consultancies pretend to.

The Profitboss works his consultants as hard as himself, selecting only those he'd have in his team if they weren't consultants.

When you run a lean and effective team, you can't afford to have all the experts you need permanently on the staff. The Profitboss gets the consultants in to supplement his team's expertise. But he gets the best: the person who provides the real thing (a contribution to profitability), the person who's been at the sharp end and actually cut a profit from the edge. The Profitboss does not tolerate consultant academics, people who have their heads in the clouds with the latest theories and who peddle new-fangled pseudo-scientific systems. They're mere entertainers.

The Profitboss finds his consultants through his network, through recommendation. It's the way most people discover the best things in life. And his network will tell him about the consultant who's got to the top by achieving top-class results.

TODAY'S STEP

Critically appraise the consultants you have engaged recently. Are they really as good as they make out? Do you really need them? Are they as good as, if not better than, the experts you have in your team?

Make sure, when you next need a consultant, to search the network and identify the best.

Avoid the large corporate consultancies: they employ battery hens.

REMEMBER

Any management consultant worth his or her salt will have been a PROFITBOSS.

Experts

Clearly differentiating between your own expertise and that of an expert is a critical executive skill

Everyone is an expert on trade unions, advertising, company communications and management, and what the experts should be doing – except the Profitboss. He's an expert on nothing except how to make profit. He's that single-minded he keeps his expertise to a single subject.

The Profitboss trusts the experts to lend their expertise to help him reach his profit-making goals. He doesn't do the engineers' jobs for them, nor tell the personnel professionals how to be more professional. He doesn't criticize the vice-president marketing's expert judgement nor pretend he could do better himself. He's humble enough to bow to their expertise.

The Profitboss even puts up with the 'five-second experts' who know better than him; for in the end he knows that these self-opinionated, self-proclaimed experts are at best opinion-mongers rather than expert decision-takers and commitment-makers.

The Profitboss recognizes and respects experts, never trying to second-guess or out-argue them. What's more, the Profitboss is aware of his own unique expertise, and that's the ability to identify if not create profitable opportunities, seize them and exploit them before anyone else does.

Whatever his original professional expertise, the Profitboss professes to only one now.

While other people waste time injecting their five-second expertise into decisions which do not call for their real expertise, the Profitboss gets ahead with his own expert profit-orientated decisions.

TODAY'S STEP

Undertake the most critical self-appraisal you've ever done. Identify your own personal areas of expertise in relation to your current job.

Become determined to develop your expertise using a self-help approach. Read the literature and learn. Talk to other experts and learn. Critically review your own experience and learn. Attend training courses and learn.

Do not attempt to broaden your boundaries by becoming an expert in everything.

Keep your mouth shut when another person talks. Listen carefully, clarify with questions if necessary, but don't challenge that person's expertise. In ninety-nine cases out a hundred, he or she knows better than you, whether you believe it or not.

REMEMBER

By definition the PROFITBOSS has only one area of expertise.

Union representatives

Without profit there would be little for a union to represent

Unions are as inadequate as the managers with whom they deal. Many perform a great disservice to their members by failing to represent their interests independently and fairly. Manipulation, propaganda, prejudice and political intrigue are often their province. The abuse of union power serves no one's interest except perhaps the egos of the officials themselves.

Many union representatives are ill-trained, ill-advised and of relatively low calibre. They are drop-outs from the mainstream of career progression. They become confused about their role and sometimes attempt to take on that of managers themselves.

The worst union representatives are those who create problems rather than solve them, who continually find fault with management rather than build on strengths.

The militant union representatives are those who fail to accept the profit motive, failing to equate profit with job security and prosperity.

The Profitboss treats union representatives in the same way as he treats any other person: with respect and with dignity. He listens carefully and reasons politely, without emotion, in evaluating objectively their argument. He doesn't automatically say 'No' and never says 'Yes' under pressure. He allows no prejudice to colour his judgement, welcoming positive suggestions and ideas put to him. Nor is he paranoic about the union trying to undermine his position or score 'victories' over him.

He takes the union representatives at face value, welcoming help and overcoming obstructions in representing his people's best interests.

He knows that by serving these interests he is in the best position to achieve what he has to achieve.

The Profitboss always tries to develop a relationship of mutual trust and respect with union representatives, ensuring that the best interests of the people are clearly understood and honestly represented.

TODAY'S STEP

Put yourself in the shoes of the union representatives with whom you deal. What are they really trying to achieve?

Why aren't you, as the boss, trying to achieve the same? Is there really a dichotomy of interests between the two?

Be honest about any prejudices that might be implanted in your mind. Is the union really trying to 'do you down', to 'deceive the company', to prove that management is incompetent?

Think carefully about your attitude towards the union and its representatives. There only is one way forward and that is to strive to work with them, not against them. In that way you can be seen to care as much for your people as the union does.

REMEMBER

The PROFITBOSS shares the same goal as a union representative: to serve the best interests of his people in serving the company.

7
PERSONNEL POLICIES FOR THE PROFITBOSS

Recruitment
Business schools
Conferences
Workshops
Profit sharing
Welfare
Overtime
Redundancy
Strikes

Recruitment

To recruit for profit you have only one option: recruit the best and pay the best

The apes some people recruit! The service these apes provide! The products they produce! You don't have to look far to see these dumb creatures crawling across the branches of many organizations today.

Ape recruitment syndrome (ARS) is a primary cause of retarded company growth and can eventually turn an organization into a jungle (if not a zoo).

If you rush recruitment, you will recruit apes. If you recruit under pressure because you are short of people, you will recruit apes.

The Profitboss goes for the best people, but never apes. It takes time to define the best and find the best. The best electronic engineers do not grow on trees, nor do excellent executives. But they do exist and they can be found. The Profitboss finds them, recruits them.

They are the people who want to escape the pet-shops they work in, or the quarantine of larger organizations. They are the specialists who are disenchanted with the simulated thrills of performing circus routines.

In recruiting the best the Profitboss gives his people the best: the best opportunities to demonstrate their real skills, the best challenge they'll ever have of making a key contribution. He gives them the best working conditions and levels of pay high enough to sustain their motivation.

The best people to recruit are those who understand the real meaning of profit and how their own unique skills relate to it. Apes don't understand profit and in any case can never keep their eye on this ball.

When recruiting, the Profitboss looks only for potential profit contribution, for profit-seeking attitudes and ability. He does not get distracted with such secondary factors as qualifications, experience and disposition.

Darwin's theory of natural selection applies to business and recruitment. It is the Profitboss who survives, the apes that lose.

TODAY'S STEP

Are you in a zoo? Do you recruit apes?

There is no excuse. You have to recruit the best, even if it means fighting an uphill battle to get personnel policies changed, to persuade your boss to pay your people more.

Prepare for your next recruitment assignment by defining 'the best'. Don't waste time writing boring job descriptions or person specifications. Just ask yourself what the best person for the job will be like. What exactly will you be looking for? Spend time defining this in as colourful terms as possible.

Find time today to start gearing your selection process to finding the best. If you go for second best (because the pressure is on to fill the job tomorrow, or because you can't afford the best) you will inevitably end up at the bottom of the heap with all the other monkeys.

REMEMBER

For the PROFITBOSS the profit-making process starts with recruitment.

Business schools

Don't be misled by business schools: you teach them their business

Business schools are excellent places for executives to learn about business – as long as they talk among themselves.

The biggest problems business schools have are their experts. These are the business academics who do expert research to produce expert theories and unworkable systems. The last thing they are are experts on making money. Why? Because most of them have never made a penny's profit in their lives.

However hard they try, business schools are divorced from the realities of business. If business is all about making money and wanting to make money, why be a lecturer in a business school? The best way to make money is to be a Profitboss, not a professor.

If executives really understand business and the motivational challenge of making profit, the last thing they will want to do is put themselves out to grass, write papers for learned journals and theorize on aspects of business they've previously failed to put into practice. Too many so-called experts in business schools are drop-outs from industry who've never succeeded in making any profit in their life: hardly a qualification for teaching business success.

The Profitboss goes to business school. But he uses the schools with caution. He'll stear clear of the lengthy and costly three-month programmes, preferring the therapy of a short three-day course where his people can receive some stimulus on how to improve their business performance.

TODAY'S STEP

Think about the business school professors you know. Would you give them a key position of accountability in your team? Do you really feel confident that they know how business works and can help you learn one or two things about it?

Talk to one or two people who've recently been to business school. Did they profit (literally) from what they learnt? If they did, find out why. Did they learn from the professors or from the other participants?

Establish which is the best business school in the country and hire its best professor at double his or her current salary. It should be a profitable experience.

REMEMBER

What they teach you at business schools, the PROFITBOSS teaches himself.

Conferences

Conferences are essential therapy

The Profitboss attends at least one external business conference every six months. He knows he will learn something from at least one of the eight speakers on the platform. The probability is that the other seven speakers will have something to learn from him. That makes it all worthwhile.

A good conference speaker will stimulate the Profitboss, help him take perspective, give him new ideas, inspire him, motivate him.

A poor conference speaker will give the Profitboss a giant ego-boost, maintaining his belief that he is equal to, if not better than, most of the top professionals in his area.

The Profitboss rarely turns down an invitation to speak at a conference, seizing the opportunity to present his company in the best light, to fine-tune his own professional skills. He prepares very thoroughly, polishing the presentation time and time again, ensuring that his speech will fit the allotted time (there's nothing worse than speakers who overrun). He has one objective: that the delegates get the very best from his personal contribution.

What's essential therapy for the Profitboss is essential therapy for his team. He ensures that they get to the best conferences and from time to time will organize his own, bringing in the best speakers. There's no better therapy.

TODAY'S STEP

Book yourself on a conference today.

You should be wise enough to select one of the best from all that promotional material floating into your in-tray.

As soon as you've fixed it, drop a note to your boss and tell him what you've done.

Your next action today is to set a standard that everyone in your team attends a conference at least once every six months. Then take action to make sure it happens.

REMEMBER

You are a PROFITBOSS when you can both excel at conferences and learn from them.

Workshops

You get more out of workshops than just work

Many executives are much too busy to give any in-depth thought to profit-making. They chase their tails.

Thinking on your feet is a great skill. But it is not enough. In a complex competitive commercial world, certain issues require in-depth thought and that requires time – time that cannot be found in a committee or a two-hour meeting with a fixed agenda. Certain issues require undivided attention, for hours on end, without interruption, without the recurring pressures of day-to-day routines.

Once every six months the Profitboss takes his team away to a hotel for a two- or three-day residential workshop, perhaps from a Thursday to Saturday. He engages a top-class consultant to help facilitate the in-depth debate on critical strategic issues: for example, employee relations, or management style, or systems policy.

The benefits of these workshops are enormous. Not only do they tackle key issues which would otherwise be neglected under every-day pressures, but they also break down barriers and strengthen team spirit and understanding.

TODAY'S STEP

Identify the strategic issue which gives you the most worry. It should be one which presents a seemingly intractable problem. Now tackle it!

Don't ignore it just because at times it seems impossible to deal with. You have to believe the problem can be resolved. It might be an industrial relations problem, or a shortage of high-calibre people in your team, or a persistent quality problem.

Set three days aside in your diary (within the next three months) to go away to a hotel with your team and tackle the issue.

To help you, engage a top-class consultant who will independently catalyse and structure the debate that you want to take place. Make sure that he (or she) clearly understands your problem. But remember: you have to believe that the seemingly intractable problem can be cracked. That's how they got a man on the moon!

REMEMBER

The PROFITBOSS secures team cohesion and commitment through the workshops he runs.

Profit sharing

The people who should share profit are the share-holders

Profit-sharing schemes are dangerous. It is a myth that they actually motivate employees to higher performance and even more profit.

The principle of 'profit sharing' has the illusion of fairness. The danger is that there are over 200 perceptions of fairness.

For a start, a company board might decide, in recession, to turn the profit-sharing scheme into a loss-sharing scheme and reduce salaries. Is that fair?

Another argument against profit sharing is that employee effectiveness is not the only determinant of profit performance. Senior management capability has a greater impact. Employees can influence profit through productivity and customer-orientation, but have no control over idiot executives who invest in crazy schemes and couldn't even market a doughnut. Is it fair to impose a dead loss on employees?

Far from being motivating, profit-sharing schemes are de-motivating. They can payout 15 per cent in a good year and nothing the next. So much for the Christmas turkey.

The Profitboss has a simple philosophy of reward and motivation. High pay and high performance are the results of managerial excellence and self-motivation. He doesn't believe that extra money motivates, whether that money be a bonus, profit sharing or a salary increase. Conversely, he knows that a drop in gross income will de-motivate.

In other words, money is no substitute for management. Nor can it permanently motivate.

In the eyes of the Profitboss, people are the company's greatest asset. But no one owns the people. Therefore, equity demands that they share in the total assets. Consequently share option schemes are a thousand better than profit-sharing schemes.

Only when employees own part of their company are they justifiably entitled to a share of the profit.

TODAY'S STEP

Think carefully about the relationship between pay, profit and performance.

First, consider yourself. Would you personally be more motivated and work more effectively if you were to receive a share of the profit at the year end? Or would you prefer a higher salary all the year round? How would you feel if your anticipated profit-sharing bonus was wiped out as a result of some crazy investment decision made by those idiots on the board?

Think carefully about what motivates you. Whatever motivates you is most likely to motivate your people too.

Having thought it through, list the pros and cons of both profit-sharing and share-option schemes, and discuss your conclusion persuasively with someone who counts.

REMEMBER

The PROFITBOSS believes in equity, shares it and profits from it.

Welfare

The source of all welfare is profit

Without profit there is little welfare. In a capitalist society you cannot escape the impact of money on your own welfare. Non-monetary factors such as time, effort and compassion are, of course, essential too, but not enough on their own.

The Profitboss puts money into welfare, motivated by a deep and genuine concern for every single person in his team. He puts money into clinics and canteens, into swimming pools and pensions, into trees, flowers and works of art to make the working environment more pleasant.

He freely gives time for the dying wife, the injured mechanic, the traumatized telephonist. You will see the Profitboss at the funeral, at the hospital, at the home of the employee in need.

He spares no effort to fix the best for his people: the best surgeon, the best tax adviser; the best recreational facilities, gymnasium, television room, squash court and so on.

It's simple. People produce more profit when they have the best welfare. The evidence is all around. Welfare is an investment, never a charity.

When people spare all their energies for the company, the Profitboss spares no little profit for their welfare. The welfare of his people is as high a priority as the welfare of his customers. The two go together.

The welfare of a company is reflected in the welfare of its people. That's how the Profitboss sees it. He needs no welfare officer – he is one.

TODAY'S STEP

Become a welfare officer for the day – and every day from now on.

Identify at least two welfare cases in your organization today. Then do something about them.

It might be the first time you send flowers, but that doesn't matter.

Check the toilets in the factory. Use them to make sure that they are working properly. That's welfare. Get the locker room repainted. Buy better lockers. That's welfare.

Eat the food in the canteen. That's welfare. If you aren't happy with it, no one else will be.

Get some welfare action today. You'll profit tomorrow.

REMEMBER

The PROFITBOSS is first and foremost a welfare officer.

Overtime

Overtime is a business disease and a social evil

Throwing money at a problem is the most ineffective form of management. Such is overtime.

Scheduling hours to be worked is one of the most basic tasks for managers. Many fail and bail themselves out with overtime.

In a civilized world, hours of work should not be continually excessive. There are other things to do in life. Overtime leads to more overtime.

Overtime kills, causes divorces and health problems. Overtime camouflages low pay rates, inefficiency, poor management and corrupt trade union practices.

The solution is simple: high basic pay for high performance during limited hours.

The Profitboss rarely uses overtime and would never rely on it. Overtime is unreliable. Plants don't operate, buses don't run, planes don't fly when you rely on overtime. Overtime pushes people too far. Full stop.

The Profitboss engages the correct number of staff to meet his planned output requirements. He assumes a standard working week or shift. If output requirements vary, he'll make the manning system flexible enough to cover peaks. Occasionally, when there's an unpredicted peak, he'll use overtime and give people time off in lieu. If there are frequent peaks, he predicts them and plans accordingly.

Overtime costs erode profit levels through inefficiency and malpractice. Overtime is a dreadful disease which companies pay for dearly. The Profitboss avoids it like the plague.

TODAY'S STEP

Cut out overtime today – or tomorrow at the latest. The unions will support you.

Your biggest priority if you suffer overtime levels in excess of 5 per cent is to improve manpower scheduling practices to achieve a 5 per cent maximum. As soon as you have achieved this, you can completely cut out overtime payments and give people time off in lieu for the occasional overtime worked.

REMEMBER

The PROFITBOSS will work overtime to cut out overtime.

Redundancy

There is no better therapy than redundancy

Shake the leaves off the tree in autumn. Cut out the dead wood so that the young new wood can grow and develop.

Not everyone should wait until the standard age to retire. A percentage grow stale prematurely, becoming disenchanted, whatever. This minority can rot the organization, festering within it. They are the people who gave their best ten years ago, and for whom nothing is good enough now. They're probably no good for you.

There is only one solution and it costs money. Often that money is the best investment a company can make.

For the Profitboss it is the most compassionate way of easing out Hugh Clarkson, the dyed-in-the-wool western region sales manager who's had enough but can't afford to admit it. It is an opportunity to expand the responsibilities of John Langley, an up-and-coming salesman getting some great results in the north. He'll make John sales manager north-western region.

For the Profitboss it is an opportunity to provide a new challenge to Steve Lockhart, the graduate trainee in Personnel who's won the confidence of the line management in engineering. The Profitboss will provide the opportunity by easing out Maureen Stilgoe, the ultra-conservative and inefficient corporate personnel manager. He'll persuade her to take redundancy and combine her job with Steve's.

There is too much sentiment and emotion about redundancy. In fact it is often something people welcome: why not get paid to take a breath of fresh air? It's an opportunity for the company to become efficient at the same time, to have new life injected into it, to bring on and develop talented younger people who might otherwise become stifled and consequently up and go.

Redundancy is not a social evil. If it is handled the 'Profitboss way', people will accept it. They'll accept the money and accept the opportunity to escape.

If there is to be charity in business, make people redundant and do it well.

TODAY'S STEP

Be courageous. Consult your boss and the top personnel person in the organization. Persuade them to develop and implement a redundancy programme, a 'one-off' to begin with. You'll be surprised how people will welcome your initiative, and how profitable it will be.

REMEMBER

When it comes to redundancy the PROFITBOSS is ruthless in decision but compassionate in execution.

Strikes

Always be prepared to take the strike

The easiest thing in the world is to say 'Yes' – especially if someone has a hand at your throat.

The Profitboss says 'No'. He doesn't cough up, cry off, cave in or collapse under pressure from the unions, no matter how fierce their attempted stranglehold.

People strike because managers say 'Yes' too often. People strike because managers say 'Yes' when they mean 'No' and 'No' when they mean 'Yes'. People strike because they see managers striking at them.

A strike is a defeat – a defeat for all. The Profitboss is prepared for a defeat but always aims to win. He wins by being fair to his people and resisting any selfish and unfair demands on their part. He does his best for his employees with the best pay increases possible. And if that is nothing he'll stick with nothing, taking the strike. Why jeopardize the company? The company is the people, and the people often commit suicide, striking at themselves. It can be a long cancerous death – a cancer of proliferated allowances, inequitable concessions, malfunctioning manning levels, destructive demarcations and unjustified jack-pots conceded under the jackboot.

The Profitboss jacks up his profit by never acquiescing to unreasonable demands. He is straight, honest and fair, always pushing for his people. If that means saying 'No', he says 'No' and means it. The unions know it. And they know not to strike.

TODAY'S STEP

Perhaps you haven't seen a strike for years. Even so, don't ignore this page. Don't become complacent.

Just ask yourself what you are doing to avoid the occurrence of a strike!

REMEMBER

The PROFITBOSS never strikes at his people.

8

THE PROFITBOSS LIFESTYLE

Home
Health
Lunches
Stress
Entertainment
Hours of work
Reading

Home

Home is a profit base

What happens at home invariably affects what happens at work. Executives who get distracted with love affairs, golfing weekends and nightly entertainment under pretence of business are in all probability not Profitbosses.

Achieving profit is no easy task, but a wife (or husband) can make it easier. The Profitboss knows how to walk that high-hung tightrope between work and pleasure, between the office and home. He would not neglect his wife in favour of his work, nor his work in favour of his wife. It is a difficult balance to achieve, and the higher up the organization one goes, the more impossible the task seems.

The Profitboss believes in effective communications at work and that requires time and effort. He also believes in effective communications at home. That requires time and effort too.

Neglected partners nag and become nuisances, their neuroses eventually having a negative impact on profit. Far better to spend time with your other half and obtain some support and understanding than escape to the club to leave your loved one isolated at home. Far better to relax in your favourite armchair, enjoy a drink with your husband (or wife) and talk through today's problems than escape with a mate for endless rounds of gin and tonic.

The Profitboss might work long hours but, come Friday, he'll leave the office at 5 p.m. and devote the weekend to the family. There is no other way.

TODAY'S STEP

At 5 o'clock forget about work and give some in-depth thought to what's happening at home.

Don't take your other half for granted. Challenge the routines that have evolved over the years. Do they serve the marriage well?

Get a babysitter for the kids this weekend (if they're that young) and take your partner away and talk through your work, your career, your lifestyle. Ask her or him straight out: 'Have we really got the balance right?'

When one in three marriages end in divorce, it is safe to assume that many couples haven't got the balance right. Work pressures are often a major factor. When the balance is wrong, the probability is that the achievement of profit will be affected adversely too.

So talk it through with your partner before it's too late. Try to maintain the right balance for both of you.

REMEMBER

For the PROFITBOSS work can never be more important than home.

Health

The health of a company is reflected in the health of its people

If you cannot care for your own body, you will not be able to care for your company. The worst decisions are made by bosses who are not fit, who never take exercise, who drink and smoke to excess and puff and pant around till midnight with overweight bellies.

Making profitable decisions requires energy, stamina and a good blood supply to the brain.

In an aggressive competitive world, stress levels are high, wearing down the weak and the wet and forcing upon them a proliferation of ailments and diseases with the consequential poor decisions and non-profitable returns.

The Profitboss is fit enough to thrive on stress, to take the never-ending pressures, to work exceptionally long hours when necessary. He encourages his people to keep healthy too, providing the necessary facilities to ease their way. A company swimming pool is a far better investment than an extravagant advertising campaign.

The Profitboss takes exercise at least three times a week and eats modest lunches, rarely consuming alcohol and then only in the evening. He takes pride in his appearance, setting a high standard to exemplify his healthy leadership style.

By caring for his own health the Profitboss cares best for the company, its people and the profits they make.

TODAY'S STEP

Seriously review your own health. Be totally honest.

- Have you had a thorough medical check-up within the last year? If not, arrange one immediately.

- How much exercise do you take? If none, start this lunch-time with a gentle walk and build up from there, taking exercise at least three times a week. As soon as you can walk well, try some very gentle jogging, running a few paces then walking.

- Review your diet. You know what's bad for you (lots of saturated fat, sugar and refined foods are the worst). Start cutting down on 'bad' foods today and consume more health-giving raw vegetables, fruits, salads, nuts, grains and pulses.

- Seriously review your alcohol consumption. Once again, deep down you know what a sensible level is (probably less than what you're consuming now). Prove to yourself how enjoyable mineral water is during business lunches.

- Look at yourself in the mirror. You should be proud of your appearance – and that means a healthy appearance.

If you are worried about being fat, fatigued, breathless, red-faced and generally unhealthy, take action today. Action today on health is guaranteed to make you feel better tomorrow. But take care! Don't overdo it first time round.

REMEMBER

The PROFITBOSS is always fit enough for healthy competition.

Lunches

The most profitable lunch is an apple, a glass of water and twenty minutes' fresh air taken with some gentle exercise

Excellent business results result from excellent relationships between company and customer. It is a myth that such relationships are best fostered over 'heavy' business lunches.

In an increasingly health-conscious world, executives from Brazil to Britain have become increasingly fed-up with luncheon excesses. A three-hour three-course lunch saturated with gin and tonic, Chablis and Rémy-Martin might be enjoyable once a month, but more frequently becomes a dangerous chore. There's no profit in that.

The Profitboss avoids frequent business lunches, trying hard to find two or three days a week when he can escape from his office at lunch-time, take a stroll, sit on a park bench and eat an apple, drink some mineral water and contemplate his next profit-making move.

However, he cannot say 'No' to all lunches. Occasionally in the pursuit of profit he has to sacrifice himself to the ordeal of a business lunch with a customer, supplier or business contact. When he does so he tries to keep the lunch simple, with one or two courses and no alcohol. He knows that a profitable deal can just as easily be struck over a caesar salad and glass of mineral water as over a T-bone steak and bottle of vintage claret.

However, he is not so undiplomatic as to resist the horrendous hospitality of overindulgent underdeveloped countries. There he'll reluctantly accept the sheep's eyes, the questionable meat and the unwashed salads medicinally disinfected with copious glasses of illicit Black Label. The last thing he'll do is tell his hosts about the headache and stomach cramps in the morning.

Nobody needs a big lunch and the Profitboss definitely doesn't need it to make a profit.

TODAY'S STEP

Now is the time to review your 'lunch discipline' and really become health-conscious.

If you are one of the majority of business executives, you probably eat too much and occasionally drink too much. Go through your diary, cutting out as many business lunches as possible, whether it be in the canteen with your colleagues or at a restaurant with an acquaintance or potential customer.

Discipline yourself to having fresh air and a simple home-prepared fruit-and-vegetable lunch two or three times a week.

If your company provides free lunches, don't be deterred from missing one occasionally and buying your own apple. Free lunches are no protection against heart disease.

REMEMBER

Lunching to excess is the biggest chore the PROFITBOSS has.

Stress

Stress is essential to success. Don't avoid it. Manage it!

You win some. You lose some. Winning brings stress; so does losing. Competition brings stress; so does your boss. The unions create stress; your customers too. Government policies add to it. The untouched in-tray can sometimes seem to be unbearably stressful. The constant telephone interruptions can appear even more so.

Talking to Ian Irvin can be exceptionally stressing. And that's no different from the uncertainty over winning the multi-million contract with Tashenu's.

You have to live with stress, with the flow of adrenalin. You cannot avoid it. Even at home there are the noisy kids, the unwelcome bills and the dripping taps.

The Profitboss manages stress effectively. He doesn't let it control him; he controls it. He develops his own personal mechanism for dealing with it. These are not the superficial ten-step techniques advocated in upmarket journals. They are, in fact, the basics. He eats properly; he exercises regularly; he reads the occasional book; he talks to people regularly and listens; he thinks; he goes home and forgets about work problems – all things that lesser mortals sacrifice when under stress.

The Profitboss reasons and gets people to reason with him. When people see reason, the stress disappears. He prioritizes and explains his priorities. Low priorities create no stress.

The Profitboss does so much and no more, knowing his limits. Thus he limits his hours, knowing that an exhausted brain creates more stress than a fresh one. Working till midnight accentuates the stress rather than relieves it. The major problem at midnight often appears insignificant in the morning. Better to take a long cool walk and see it that way than lose perspective in the weary hours of the night.

When it's all happening and the stress seems unbearable, the Profitboss bears it. It takes just five seconds for him to realize that there are only so many hours in the working day to establish the key priorities and apply his mind to them. It takes just five seconds for him to eliminate the stress.

By controlling the priorities, the Profitboss controls the stress.

It is uncertainty that creates stress. The Profitboss reduces the uncertainty. If it's outside his control, why worry? Better concentrate on what you can control and get on with it. There's little stress in that.

TODAY'S STEP

Develop your own method for dealing with stress.

The best way is to be 'normal'. Eat well and relax every day. You can only do so much at work, so don't try to do any more.

In the hours you allocate for work, sort out your priorities, re-ordering them when unforeseen circumstances arise. If something outside your control is creating stress, forget it: there's nothing you can do about it.

Concentrate on the things you can do well within a reasonable working day, establishing the priorities as you go along.

Don't resort to alcohol to relieve your stress. Just try doing the normal things. That way you will keep stress to a minimum. The problems will be resolved without your adding to them.

If you really do feel under stress, find five minutes to sit quietly and relax. Try reading these pages again and again.

REMEMBER

You will see the PROFITBOSS at his best under stress.

Entertainment

Entertainment should never be used as an end in itself

There is no such thing as a free meal. If you believe that a glass of wine will sell a motor car, you are underestimating the customer.

The Profitboss devotes his time and energy to the customer relationship, not the wine. That relationship generates belief: customer belief in the product, customer belief in the supplier. Entertainment does not generate belief but merely facilitates the relationship.

If he has any choice, the Profitboss will share a simple lunch with his customers. Most of his customers, no matter how fat, would prefer that too.

Boxes at Wimbledon, golfing weekends and ski holidays at Les Arcs are on the boundaries of business entertainment and business corruption. The Profitboss steers clear of such indulgence, for in the end everyone pays dearly for the privilege of the few. If you have to buy a customer with lavish entertainment, you might as well buy your way out of every problem. That's no way to manage.

Entertainment should be simple hospitality, no more. If you eat in the staff restaurant at lunch-time, take your customers there too. Let them see you and your company as you are: in that way they'll believe in you and your people.

The Profitboss never buys customer belief, for he knows that in the end both he and the customer would pay dearly.

TODAY'S STEP

Starting today and starting with yourself, be totally ruthless in attacking all expenditure on entertainment. Challenge it and challenge it again until it's at a bare minimum.

If you want to get fat, do it at home. Profit comes from slim-line companies and Profitbosses who keep a slim-line entertainment account. But don't starve your customers in the process – there's no profit in that either. Genuine hospitality is the order of the day, not lavish entertainment.

REMEMBER

Business entertainment is hard work. The PROFITBOSS therefore seeks his entertainment outside work.

Hours of work

The price of inefficiency is long hours at work

I used to believe in the Protestant work ethic, in the virtue of a regular twelve-hour working day, deluding myself that this was the only way to achieve excellent business results, kidding myself that I actually enjoyed going home exhausted on Friday evening, taking with me a whole bundle of weekend paperwork.

Then I saw one of my colleagues die from a heart attack and two others crack up under the strain. I saw marriages uncouple. I met executives who knew the inside of a Concorde better than their own back yard, who had telephones stuck permanently to their ears.

Workaholism is an unpleasant disease. Executives suffer, families suffer, companies suffer.

The Profitboss balances the priorities, never putting work before everything, nor everything before work. Family, friends, health and relaxation have high priority in his life. The Profitboss makes sure that he finds time for them all, never espousing twelve-hour working days as a routine. He knows that the most successful companies encourage an eight-hour day at all levels, frowning upon overtime, whether paid or unpaid. Crises are an exception, of course, but crises are rare.

It is not without reason that contracts of employment in most civilized countries are geared to a working week of between thirty-seven and forty-four hours. The Profitboss has seen the effect of prolonged hours of work, has seen the fatigue, the bad decisions, the poor-quality workmanship and the poor service. He has seen the reduction in profit.

Long hours are often a reflection of an organization's bureaucratic inefficiency. The Profitboss goes for efficiency and eight fresh hours at work a day. He takes pride in clearing his desk at 5.30 p.m. and leaving for home. He encourages his people to do the same.

Occasionally he will get in early to see the morning shift or stay late for the night shift. But then he will have no compunction in taking Friday afternoon off to go shopping with his spouse.

TODAY'S STEP

Have you put in additional hours at work over the last few days? Has it become routine to stay at your desk till 6.30 p.m.? If so, why? Is it just for the sake of appearances because everyone else does?

Try to discipline yourself to work contracted hours only. If you want to indulge, get in half an hour early.

Try to set the example for the rest of your organization. You know that if you kill yourself with fatigue, you'll have no hours left at all.

REMEMBER

The PROFITBOSS only puts in additional hours at exceptional times.

Reading

It is all there at your finger-tips if only you could read it

The easiest thing to do is stop reading, to find that a whole year has passed without even a glimpse of a business book.

When you've ploughed your way through all that mail, glanced at each report and discarded the promotional bumph, the last thing you might want to do is read a book or journal on management.

The Profitboss does. He seeks stimulus and perspective from the best management writers, profiting from their profit-making experiences. The rest is rubbish, of course, full of dreary words, academic jargon and mundane thoughts. Most management writers lack inspiration and have nothing to say. The Profitboss discovers the exceptions. He reads the reviews, scans the bookshops and takes recommendations from his colleagues. The exceptions cost a percentage of most business training courses and are worth much more.

The Profitboss spends at least one hour a week reading the best about business. When travelling, it's even more. He will have learnt from Iacocca, pursued excellence, been up the organization and spent one minute as a manager. He will know the IBM way and even what it takes to be a Superboss.

He'll build a department library from the business books he and his people buy. His secretary will administer it. Once or twice a year he'll go even further and invite a business writer to come and talk to his people. That way everyone will read and learn.

TODAY'S STEP

Prepare a reading schedule of business books. Then start reading – set aside at least one hour today. Take notes and take notice.

It's just another good way to learn how to make profit.

REMEMBER

The PROFITBOSS reads for profit.

9

WHAT THE PROFITBOSS AVOIDS

Job descriptions
Large filing systems
The board
Committees
Sub-contractors
Status
The personality cult
Sex
Management fashions
Set formulae
Crisis panics

Job descriptions

The shorter the job description, the greater the profit potential

Nobody profits from lengthy job descriptions. They are a drag on the organization, wasting precious management time, consuming vast amounts of paper and producing paralytic rather than positive effects.

Job descriptions never make for exciting reading, no matter how exciting the job (and the Profitboss always aims to make his people's jobs exciting). Most job descriptions are bland, boring, totally devoid of colour and – worse still – frequently devoid of real meaning.

For a company to profit, everyone must have a job that can be clearly and succinctly described in less than forty words. Only in that way can a job be effectively understood. In keeping the description of the job to a few generalized but well-understood statements, a manager can well flex the boundaries of that job to meet the dynamic thrusts of the world around and to maximize contribution.

The Profitboss doesn't squander precious time writing and reading lengthy job descriptions. For him jobs are like people: changeable but capable of immense development. Long rigid job descriptions serve only to limit profit contribution and inhibit the vital development of the job. Boundary changes can be readily incorporated into broad-based jobs with succinct descriptions, but will produce dissent if the job description has been negotiated into a thirty-point legal document. In the latter case every change tends to become a pay issue and another bureaucratic burden on the organization.

The Profitboss doesn't fill the filing cabinet with job descriptions. He just makes sure that everyone in his team knows the job they have to do and the accountabilities they hold. He doesn't need reams of paper for that.

TODAY'S STEP

Tear up all the job descriptions in your area and re-write each in less than forty words. If you have eight people in your immediate team, this should take you less than one hour.

Make a vow never to write another long job description. If you can't conceptualize a job in less than forty words, you won't be able to conceptualize the job clearly at all.

Union resistance is no excuse for not making profit, nor is it an excuse for long legalistic job descriptions.

REMEMBER

The PROFITBOSS has forty words for every job, no more.

Large filing systems

The profitability of an organization is in inverse proportion to the number of filing cabinets it has

Filing systems were invented for managers with empty heads. Ninety per cent of filing cabinets are repositories for useless bits of paper containing useless bits of information.

The larger the filing system, the less likely you are to find that nugget of hidden gold when you want it. There are stronger words for bureaucratic waste, yet many organizations continue to tolerate the accumulation of managerial excretions, creating unseen dung-heaps in corridors of metal. There always is a better use, for no one really needs that faded 1976 memo.

The Profitboss profits from a light-weight portable filing system. It's called his brain, and what he can't store there he stores in a single cabinet backed with a simple personal computer and word processor. He's not that intolerant that he doesn't recognize the need for personnel records, legal contracts and key reports to be filed away. But what he doesn't do is stuff his secretary silly with volumes of useless memos to be re-stuffed into overflowing filing cabinets. Bulky filing systems never work, they just stop work.

In a dynamic world you cannot record and store away every little memo, every little documented change, every little recorded thought, every little written opinion, every little piece of regurgitated data.

Dynamism is the hallmark of a Profitboss, not bureaucracy.

TODAY'S STEP

Take out all your frustrations on your filing cabinets. Tear them apart. Destroy every single memo you discover inside, together with 90 per cent of everything else you find.

Ring up a dealer and sell off at least two-thirds of your filing cabinets. The additional space will be invaluable (pot plants are far more attractive than filing cabinets).

Explain to your secretary what you are doing as you fill up the waste bins. Otherwise you might have to apply the smelling salts.

REMEMBER

For every document the PROFITBOSS puts into the filing system he puts a further hundred into the waste bin.

The board

There is no place for a Profitboss on the board

Boards should only have one role: as independent representatives of the interests of the company's share-holders.

The last thing any board should attempt to do is manage, which is just as well, because most board members are totally incompetent as managers.

The board is there to ensure that the share-holders achieve the best return on their investment. To that extent a board should independently review profit progress to date as well as carefully evaluate and then endorse strategic recommendations made by the senior executive team which will have a long-term and substantial impact on profit.

If a board is unhappy with the profit progress being made, it should change the management rather than attempt to do the managing itself.

The Profitboss likes action, and by definition he never sees action on the board. The Profitboss likes to lead people to profitable achievement, and by definition boards never lead anyone anywhere. The Profitboss therefore has no desire to be elected to the board.

Boards are cumbersome bureaucratic legal bodies best left to the cumbersome bureaucratic legal task of representing share-holders' interests. As soon as a board attempts to interfere with management tasks it's a fair bet that profits will decline. Far better to get a team of Profitbosses on board and delegate the management to them.

TODAY'S STEP

If you are a board member, send a copy of this book to your senior executive team, highlighting these two pages with the annotation: 'I'm sure you'll agree'.

If you are not a board member, send a copy of this book to every board member you know, highlighting these two pages with the annotation: 'I'm sure you'll agree'.

REMEMBER

The PROFITBOSS manages for profit, not for a place on the board.

Committees

The last thing most committees do is commit, let alone contribute to profit

Committees are the antithesis of professional management. They tend to be time-wasting, inefficient, bureaucratic and mere platforms for inept 'five-second' experts to voice their opinions on subjects about which they know little. There is no profit in that.

For many incompetent managers, membership of a committee is a status symbol, presenting an opportunity to join an 'inner circle' or 'secret clan' of the privileged few.

Most committees have at least thirty-five items on the agenda and ramble on from 9 a.m. till lunch-time with inadequate, uninspired, and untrained chairmanship. They get through relatively little business and are relatively ineffective at making decisions. (Try identifying a decision from the minutes of a committee! It's like looking for a needle in a haystack.)

Committees are places where you can see people snoozing, picking their noses and pretending to be interested in subjects which are of no interest to them. The best thing about committees are the coffee-breaks!

The Profitboss avoids committees like the plague. At worst he will limit himself to two a month, one run by his boss (which the Profitboss might well have to suffer) and one he might run for his own team to review progress. This he will limit to half an hour.

If he wants to consult people, he won't do it through committees. He'll get his people together in other ways. And he'll do the same to achieve commitment and to communicate – he'll never use committees. They are too inflexible for that. In fact, they are a disease.

TODAY'S STEP

Abolish three out of four committees today.

Then get together with your team to agree on the best approach to communications, consultation and obtaining commitment in your area. (Anyone who suggests another committee should be sent to serve for twelve months on the company's welfare, safety or canteen committee!)

Your second action today is to resign from other people's committees. You can explain later. (It will become item no. 36 on the agenda, and in any event you have more important things to do.)

REMEMBER

The greater the number of committees in a company, the fewer the number of PROFITBOSSES.

Sub-contractors

Why let sub-contractors profit from you?

The Profitboss takes a tough line on sub-contracting – a money line. He has no sentiment. Providing his standards and requirements are met, he'll get the cleaning done by outsiders if it's cheaper. The same applies to systems programming, catering, management training, publicity, security and many other key activities. In fact, in his wildest dreams the Profitboss sometimes wishes he was a one-man band, sub-contracting out all the company's operations including selling. In this day and age there are always people keen to do the job for you. And if they are keener than your militant unionized staff, why not let them?

The answer is profit. Why let the sub-contractor take the profit? Better to get the job done cost-effectively through your own people and share the profit with them. There's little reason why you need to sub-contract cleaning, transportation or other functions unless you can't be bothered to manage. The Profitboss can hire cleaners just as cheaply as a sub-contractor, and they'll take more pride in identifying with him and the company than with some boss once removed.

Sub-contracting is a matter of money and commitment. Better to have your own people committed to a contract rather than sacrifice their jobs and an element of profit to an outside sub-contractor.

The only exception is when you need unique expertise not required on a permanent basis. Then the Profitboss will sub-contract out to the experts. Otherwise he'll keep the work in house, and get it done more cost-effectively than by using any sub-contractor.

TODAY'S STEP

Cut down on sub-contractors today. The only justification for sub-contracting is if you need to hire in some specialist expertise on a temporary basis.

Sub-contracting is often a substitute for poor management. It is an excuse for not getting pay systems sorted out, for neglecting the problem of de-motivated staff.

Sub-contracting is a blunt axe for chopping out militant unions who've persistently exploited dull management.

If you are razor-sharp, you'll cut out the sub-contractors today and get the job done in house. This will raise morale and, of course, profit levels. It must be the case if you're paying a profit to the sub-contractor.

Put the sub-contractor's profit back into your own company's pocket today.

REMEMBER

The PROFITBOSS only sub-contracts out as a last resort.

Status

Status is a cosmetic poison

Everyone wants recognition and appreciation. The danger is that many seek that recognition and appreciation through status rather than contribution and achievement.

A grand presidential title, a large company car and expensive luxury office bring little credit to a status-conscious executive who has achieved no more than a political victory in the rat-race. Taking a mineral-water lunch with your colleagues in a secluded senior executive dining room can divorce you from the real contributors as much as from the contribution you seek. Privilege parking places yield little profit, while special perks can precipitate horrendous losses. When one person has a company car, every one will want a company car.

The danger of rewarding people through status is that status becomes an end in itself. And that can put an end to an organization.

The Profitboss concentrates on the real ends of his business. He gets his satisfaction from contributing to high levels of profit, not from parading any status symbol the company cares to give him. He doesn't mind whether he's given the title of president, director or manager – these are mere status-labels. All he minds about is making more and more profit.

He knows that the pursuit of status can consume vast amounts of people's time and efforts with the negative result of demoralizing everyone around. The Profitboss is not interested in status. He parks with his team, eats with his team and uses the same toilets as his team. He takes care not to differentiate himself from his team in any way by status. He wants everyone pointing in the same direction, and that means a common culture and a common status.

The Profitboss reflects differential contribution through differential pay. That's where the value is. In no other way will he differentiate.

TODAY'S STEP

Cause a revolution in your company: start a campaign to discard all status symbols.

Persuade the people at the top to replace company cars with a salary equivalent. Persuade them to eliminate privilege parking, abolish executive dining facilities and open up directors' toilets to everyone. Furthermore, persuade them to allow everyone to fly the same class of air travel.

Some people might go for your head to begin with, but within five years you'll find that you are the most popular person around.

In any case, if the food and conditions in the staff restaurant aren't good enough for you, why should they be good enough for the person who cleans your office?

REMEMBER

The PROFITBOSS displays no status symbols.

The personality cult

The achievement of profit is independent of personality

There is too much emphasis on personality in modern-day profit management. It takes all types, not clones to contribute.

Business attitudes are important, business skills are important, business behaviour is important. But personality is not. Profit-making attitudes, skills and behaviour can be acquired, personality cannot.

The Profitboss is totally objective in making people decisions in business. Personality is an area of subjectivity he avoids, despite the proliferation of personality tests. He ignores the profiles these tests produce, having yet to see a meaningful correlation between personality and business success.

The Profitboss will therefore not make decisions based on personality, whether it be Millie Clark's shyness or Billy Boyle's extrovert tendencies. That's too subjective. In looking at people he is looking at profit potential and the attitudes and skills relating to that.

Millie Clark might not be able to sell, but that is a 'business skill' decision the Profitboss has to make, not one of personality. Billy Boyle might not be the best manager of people, but that is a 'management development' issue, not one of personality.

Profit-making is business. The Profitboss divorces the business from the personality, developing the team's business skills rather than their personalities. 'Being the best' and 'customer service excellence' are attitudes of mind, not functions of personality. Selling computers well and producing baked beans efficiently are functions of skill, not of personality.

The Profitboss always goes for the best. That means the best skills and the most positive attitudes. It does not mean the best personality. There is no such thing. Both a shy person and an extrovert person can show positive attitudes and exhibit highly developed business skills.

TODAY'S STEP

Reject all personality tests from your management practice. Destroy the files and eliminate any thoughts you have regarding people's personality. This will enable you to concentrate on the business of making profit and on the skills and attitudes of the people contributing to it.

When customers judge your counter staff they judge attitude, skill, efficiency, service standards and courtesy. They do not judge personality, nor do they use personality tests. You shouldn't either.

Forget personality today. Think 'profit' instead.

REMEMBER

The PROFITBOSS is a personality only because of the profit he makes.

Sex

Sex and profit are commercially incompatible

Nature must take its course. In a civilized world that course is controlled. Sex in the office, or elsewhere at work, leads to a loss of control. Even thinking about sex at work is a distraction from making profit.

Furthermore, the controlled use of sex when, for example, attractive women are depicted in advertisements and on business calendars, ultimately shows a lack of respect for the customer and detracts from the essence of the product you are trying to sell, which is not sex. If it were, it would be prostitution.

Loving sex is joy. There is little joy in a clandestine relationship in the office: the occasional thrill, perhaps, but no more. Loving relationships thrive in an open and honest environment, not in dark rooms behind locked doors.

Similarly the products and services you sell should be openly and honestly advertised, packaged and displayed. They should not be clothed in sexual disguises with near-naked women pretending to sell everything but the product itself. You might try to sell dreams but in the end people don't buy them. In fact, people buy the real thing, so don't attempt to divorce your products from this reality. No product or service in a respectable world brings sexual satisfaction, so don't equate your product with it.

It might be heresy to say this in a modern world, but the Profitboss is a puritan. Home is far from the office. And it is in the privacy of his home that he demonstrates the ultimate love for his partner.

Back at the work-place the Profitboss has only one goal in mind. And it is not sex. He might have sexual desires, he might find certain people attractive. But at the work-place the pursuit of profit allows him no time to be distracted with personal pursuits better attended to elsewhere.

TODAY'S STEP

Become a work-place puritan right now.

The pursuit of sexual satisfaction at work will completely rob you of any job satisfaction. So forget about that attractive person on the floor below. Concentrate on the task at hand, which is contributing to profit today.

If you are single and the potentially perfect partner comes face to face with you at work, perhaps you have no option but to start a relationship. However, conduct it openly and honestly well away from work and not during work hours.

Remember that you will put your job at risk if you allow your partner to distract you at work.

REMEMBER

When it comes to achieving profit the PROFITBOSS keeps sex out of mind, out of sight and out of the way.

Management fashions

Profit management cannot be fashioned

Fashions are skin-deep. Managing people for profit goes deeper than MBO, performance appraisal, quality circles, T-groups, outward bound training, psychometric tests or whatever the latest fashionable approach to management is.

Fashions cover up the imperfections, distract attention from them. People-management systems, however fashionable, will never resolve deep-rooted people-management problems. MBO might make your management practice look more beautiful, but it won't help you achieve your objectives unless, of course, your people really understand the significance of objective-setting – in which case they wouldn't need MBO. The same applies to other fashionable approaches to management.

At best, management fashions provide a stimulus for examining the fundamental principles of profit management. At worst, they are a façade hiding the worst excesses of management. At best, management fashions can facilitate effective profit management. At worst, they become a time-consuming bureaucratic substitute for the real thing.

The Profitboss does not pander to fashions. He sets objectives without yielding to the latest fashion for doing so. He appraises his people's performance without the use of expensive printed paper. He selects his people using common sense, not graphology nor 'Delta-factor' personality tests. He gets his team working together without recourse to expensive T-groups or questionable outward bound training.

The Profitboss wears no management lipstick, does not indulge in 'flavours of the month' or use magic wands.

The Profitboss is not fashion-conscious in being management-wise.

TODAY'S STEP

Personally challenge the latest management fashion. Do you really believe it's necessary? Do you really believe that the performance appraisal system (currently so fashionable) is helping achieve profit? If you do, carry on with it. If you don't, tear up the appraisal forms today and find a better way to assess performance and make profit.

The latest fashion for managing people successfully might be fine, but it must be based on some fundamental principles of people management. If you don't believe in the fundamentals underlying the latest fashion, go back to 'square one' and carefully examine (and develop) the basic principles on which you manage for profit.

As soon as you have established these, systematically evaluate any management fashion being paraded around. Will it really help? If you're not sure, it's best you avoid the fashion and stick to the basics.

REMEMBER

The PROFITBOSS has his own bible and that's not fashionable.

Set formulae

If there were a formula for making profit, we'd all be millionaires

There is no formula for making profit, yet many executives think there is. They go to business school, read management books and consult consultants as they try to work out the correct equation. They are modern-day alchemists.

Finance people are the worst. They have a simple formula: cut costs and increase profits. It rarely works.

Making profit is all about taking risks, and there is no formula for that – just gut feeling, courage and common sense. Systematic evaluation and forecasting can minimize risks but never eliminate them. The executives who try to wring out the risk from forecasts, re-working and re-working the numbers in the equations until they produce a profit, at best plan for mediocrity.

While these people are sitting on committees hammering the plans into a synthetic budget which nobody can achieve, the Profitboss is out on the street making a profit, putting up prices, discounting prices, pushing the market, pulling the market. He's got a flair (not a formula) for knowing what his customers want and ensuring that they get it.

When he's not out on the street, he's in house talking, walking, explaining, consulting, listening and deciding. There's no formula for that, no formula for talking with the fixers, grinders and carriers of this world. But there's profit in it.

TODAY'S STEP

Clear out those dusty shelves and get rid of those dreary, formalized, formula-style, 'how-to' business manuals. Be ruthless: any manual containing formulae and procedures for making profit should be disposed of.

Be positive and take a risk. Trust your gut feeling, intuition and common sense. Forget your formula today and put your energy into fostering flair and entrepreneurialism in your team and in yourself.

REMEMBER

The PROFITBOSS has only one formula for success and that's his secret.

Crisis panics

A crisis is the best test of strength you'll ever have

In normal circumstances it is difficult to know the limits of one's own capability, let alone those of the organization. A crisis presents the Profitboss with an opportunity to learn about these limits, about his own strengths and weaknesses as well as those of others around. It is an opportunity to expose and mend the gaps in the fence, the cracks in the wall and the holes in the ground.

An unfortunate accident in the solvent plant, a fire in the warehouse, a large-scale burglary, the loss of a key client, some bad publicity over a defective product, an unexpected but substantial price increase on raw materials can all present a crisis to a company, and most companies have such crises from time to time.

Whatever the crisis, the Profitboss takes command. As soon as he knows about it he goes into automatic 'crisis mode', remaining cool and placing top priority on obtaining the key facts and assessing the options to minimize damage to the company and its people while resolving the problem. In the initial 'crisis mode' little else will receive his attention. As soon as the situation is under control, however, he will return to the normal routine and his people will follow.

Even so, while in 'crisis mode' he will have his eye on the organization, carefully watching how the systems cope, how emergency procedures work and, most importantly, how the people around him take the strain and react. All the while he will be learning. Why did the crisis occur in the first place? Could it have been avoided? How is it being handled? When the crisis is over he'll sit down with his team and review all the factors and identify what future improvements can be made.

Fires are better prevented than put out and that's the way the Profitboss views it, preferring to learn from the problem rather than go on a witch-hunt and blame someone for it.

TODAY'S STEP

Imagine the worst. Imagine a major crisis in your area of responsibility. Do you have a contingency for it? Having got a vivid picture in your mind, spell out the steps that have to be taken to bring the crisis under control and resolve it.

How will you take command? Are the necessary emergency procedures and systems in place? Will you be able, at any point in time, to get hold of key people?

Look back at any crises which occurred over the last few years. What did you learn from them?

Finally, you must always ask yourself, 'What could have been done to prevent the crisis?'

REMEMBER

The PROFITBOSS learns from every crisis, taking profit on the way.

10

FINANCE AND THE PROFITBOSS

Budgets
Revenue
Costs
Expenses
Investment
Cash-flow

Budgets

A budget is not a game of back-protection but a commitment to profit

The games managers play, budgetary games:

- Padding the budget with hidden costs.

- Sliding slack up their sleeves.

- Indulging in year-end spending sprees to force up next year's budgeted expenditure.

- Depressing revenue forecasts to produce an easily achieved budget.

- Negotiation rituals with finance, putting 10 per cent more in to negotiate 10 per cent back.

The Profitboss doesn't tolerate this. He knows that if you play games with budgets, costs go up and profits go down.

The Profitboss comes clean: with his boss, with his people, with his colleagues. His budgets are clean too. He puts into them what he genuinely believes he needs to achieve the required levels of profit, and he can justify each figure.

He requires the same of his people. He understands their need for contingency, for cover, and accepts a reasonable amount.

The Profitboss never manipulates his budgets to show a paper profit he knows he cannot achieve, nor does he massage his costs for reasons of comfort and insurance against poor performance. He plays no budgetary games nor does he tolerate finance people playing games with him. His budget is a cast-iron commitment. That means a commitment to every figure in it, a commitment to taking a risk to achieve the budgeted outputs. It is a commitment to profit.

He expects no less of his people. If they can't commit to high rates of profit, perhaps they should be working for a second-rate firm which plays budgetary games.

TODAY'S STEP

Pull out your budget and critically review each line on it. Can you still justify each figure? Be honest with the finance people (who's running the show, you or they?). Release any slack and improve your profit projections immediately.

Conversely, don't let the finance people brow-beat you into figures you know you cannot achieve.

Inject some integrity into your budget, but never play politics with it.

The last thing you should do is go on a spending spree at the end of the year to justify this year's budget and enhance next year's.

REMEMBER

The PROFITBOSS budgets for success and it's a commitment.

Revenue

Revenue generation should be an obsession with every single company employee

Revenue is very visible. Tom Knight sees it in the occupancy levels in his hotels. Sandy Selhurst sees it in the shelf-space her product is getting across the region. Bert Burnell sees it in the number of passengers travelling on each of his routes.

Revenue is something you can get an instant 'feel' for, something which excites and stimulates. Getting the revenue figures on a Monday morning can be as exhilarating as attending a top-class athletics meeting. Focusing on revenue is a thousand times more positive and productive than focusing on costs, which can prove debilitating and negative.

The Profitboss puts the spotlight on revenue. He makes sure that Dave Wynters, Stan Parsons and Eileen Tucker are totally conversant with the revenue status, if possible on a daily rather than weekly basis. He gets them to think 'money', to think 'cash-flow', to think 'sales revenue'. He wants them to share in the excitement of an excellent revenue week.

By persuading everyone to think 'revenue', the Profitboss encourages everyone to contribute to revenue generation. The engineering manager who chats warmly to the customers has a revenue impact, as does the quality control manager who spies on the competition, as does the production director who pulls out all the stops to achieve an impossible deadline. The Profitboss and his team never stop thinking revenue.

TODAY'S STEP

Propagandize revenue. Flag revenue. Make sure that everyone in your team knows what's happening on the revenue front today, this week, this month. (If you don't know yourself, find out.)

Go out of your way to ensure that everyone appreciates their own personal contribution to revenue. If they don't have an impact on revenue, why are they there?

REMEMBER

The PROFITBOSS sees his salary in the revenue.

Costs

A cost is an investment

Costs have got themselves a terrible name, mainly because narrow-minded finance people have concentrated on reducing them in an effort to increase profit.

Costs have the reputation of being bad for profit. Finance people, being relatively simple-minded, have only learnt subtraction in their arithmetic lessons at school, and that's what traditional cost control is. They find multiplication quite difficult, and that's what investment is.

The Profitboss is a 'multiplier'. He sees the cost of the trees planted near the entrance to the company's building branching into profit. He sees the cost of training the receptionist to smile multiplying into a thousand money-making opportunities. He sees the cost of effective management training as nothing against the true cost of incompetent management.

The Profitboss eliminates any costs that cannot be perceived as investments. He subjects every item of expenditure within his control to the question: 'What is the investment opportunity if I approve of this expenditure?'

He encourages his people to think in the same way. 'Jane,' he'll ask as he signs an expense claim, 'why did you invest in this trip to see Pierre Broger in Paris?' Similarly, when he visits the south-east region, he will want to know why so many sales people are investing their time in the office rather than out on the road selling.

Your view of costs depends on your attitude. Viewed positively, they are an investment. Viewed negatively, they are a waste. In approving costs the Profitboss sees nothing but a profitable investment opportunity.

TODAY'S STEP

Think carefully about every expenditure decision you make, whether it be an external telephone call or sanctioning an exhibition tour. What is the investment opportunity? Is there a better one?

If you can't answer, don't make a decision. Why spend money on things you can't relate to profit? You may as well cut costs.

REMEMBER

Every cost is a profit opportunity for the PROFITBOSS.

Expenses

No one profits from expenses

The myth is that people do profit from expenses. The more you try to, the more corrupt you and your organization are likely to be. A climate of distrust, dishonesty and mutual exploitation will be created and no one profits from that.

Rest it on your conscience if you take the airport bus and charge the taxi. Rest it on your conscience if you wine and dine your lover and claim client entertainment. The fact you feel the company is exploiting you with long hours of work and low pay is no reason to exploit the company with expense abuse. Two wrongs do not make a profit.

Methods of controlling expenses are a mere reflection of the levels of trust in an organization. The more bureaucratic these controls are, the less trust there is. In a perfect world there is no expense control (everyone is that honest). But we don't live in a perfect world.

Many companies institutionalize dishonesty and exploitation of expenses by paying daily allowances. Governments encourage it further with excessive taxation on pay: 'Expense your way around that!'

The approach of the Profitboss is simple. He always signs the expenses form in front of the claimant. He always looks the claimant in the eye. He knows and so does the claimant. These are the honest facts. The Profitboss puts his trust in his people.

TODAY'S STEP

Confirm your resolve to be totally honest in claiming expenses. (The slightest dishonesty on your part will be reflected in the dishonesty of your team.)

Confirm your resolve to minimize expenses and not exploit them. (Why eat an expensive meal when away if you're happy with a cheese sandwich at home?)

Start a routine whereby you sign expenses claim forms face to face when you have your monthly meeting with each team-member. Always look the person in the eye before signing. Don't be afraid occasionally to challenge claims for taxi fares and expensive meals. When you trust your people, they can stand the challenge.

REMEMBER

The PROFITBOSS keeps his expenses to the minimum necessary to do his job.

Investment

You have to invest more than money to make profit

Life is full of investment opportunities. If you don't seize one this minute, the Profitboss will, and he'll be streets ahead of you tomorrow.

Investing for profit is not just a matter of the hardware you buy and how productively you use it. The Profitboss sees his time and energy as a primary investment source. He sees his people in the same way.

Many companies invest millions in new machinery, high technology and computerized equipment and then stall on investing a few thousand on training their managers. That's poor investment.

The Profitboss puts priority on investing in people as well as in property and plant. When he hires Sally Allport as assistant treasurer, Roberto Luciano to manage International Sales or Laurie Vickers to lead Development Engineering, he is seizing an investment opportunity. When he fires Craig Norman for incompetent management, it is in response to an investment opportunity.

The Profitboss invests in the best. He invests his time and effort as well as money in getting the best people and getting the best from them, in getting the best equipment and getting the best from it.

Every minute of his working day is a minute he invests in making profit. Every time he speaks to a colleague, a team-member or a customer, he is seizing an investment opportunity. Everytime he writes a report, makes a decision, goes for a walk, he is seizing an investment opportunity. He is investing his time, his experience, his energy. He has only one investment goal.

Investing in new fork-lift trucks, word-processors and robots is essential, but there are other key elements to the Profitboss's investment strategy.

TODAY'S STEP

Evaluate the investments you have made recently. For example, try to evaluate your own personal investment in your team.

Then look at your customers. How much time have you invested in them? Don't forget your production facilities, your office accommodation, your transport fleet. What have you invested in these?

Create half an hour's time today to review additional investment opportunities in your area. Then make the investment and profit from it.

Always differentiate between the short-term and long-term investment pay-offs. Never sacrifice the latter for the former.

REMEMBER

The PROFITBOSS is a prize investor. No one else shows better dividends.

Cash-flow

Cash-flow is the barometer of a company's fortunes

Companies go crazy over cash-flow. They screw their suppliers, screw their people and eventually screw themselves with it. You can apply the tourniquet once in a life-time, but more often it can be fatal.

The simplest test of a company's fortunes is to find out how quickly they pay their suppliers. Macho finance people who delight in delaying payments for months on end are the prime cause of the terminal disease 'arterial cashosis' (blockage of the cash-flow arteries).

The best companies pay up within thirty days and take pride in doing so. The Profitboss seeks profit by maintaining excellent relations with suppliers, staff, customers and colleagues alike. As soon as you start screwing them up on cash issues, delaying payments, these relationships deteriorate.

The Profitboss never sits on expenses claims or invoices; nor does he issue instructions restricting supplies of cash.

Cash-flow manipulation is symptomatic of far deeper problems in the organization, problems which the Profitboss takes action to avoid. Revenue generation is his first priority. He and his team are simple-minded about getting out and getting cash flowing in from the customer.

The thirty days' standard he applies to his suppliers is the thirty days' standard he expects from his customers. He makes sure that they know it. It's the only way he'll do business. To invest your suppliers' money and take the interest yourself verges on the immoral. It's an unscrupulous way of exploitative discounting.

For the Profitboss, concentrating on positive cash-flow is ten times more effective than dabbling with negative cash-flow.

TODAY'S STEP

Unless you work in Accounts, the probability is that you don't even know how quickly your company pays your suppliers, or how quickly your customers pay you. Payments are probably dealt with by some junior clerk who applies his or her own interpretation of what the company wants.

Find out today what your Accounts Department is doing in terms of cash-flow. Furthermore, assess the impact of their cash-flow practices on your own relationship with customers and suppliers alike. Do not take it for granted that Accounts will be paying up the way you want or that suppliers will stay with you if they don't get paid on time. Insensitive handling of cash-flow by Accounts might just be the last straw to turn a key person away from you when you need him or her the most.

Don't rely on your Accounts Department to manage the cash-flow for you. They might just mismanage it. Be a Profitboss today and start managing the cash-flow for your own area of profitability.

REMEMBER

Flowing cash is the life blood of the PROFITBOSS.

11
THE PROFITBOSS IN THE MARKETPLACE

Competitors
Design identity
Marketing
Publicity
Selling
Customers
Contacts
Selling on
Complaints
Prospects

Competitors

If you had no competitors, you would not be in business

For a start, you have to know who your competitors are. Second, you have to respect them. Third, you have to believe that they can do as well as you. Finally, you have to believe that you can do better than them. Being competitive is an attitude of mind. Competition produces progress and success.

The Profitboss is a competitor. Every opportunity he loses is one the competition will seize. Every sales outlet his people fail to visit is one the competition will visit. Every sub-standard piece of merchandise is one the competition will replace.

The Profitboss knows that if his people don't smile at customers, his competitors' people will. He knows that if his products don't get there on time, his competitors' will.

Complacency is endemic in industry today. The manifestation of complacency is poor service. To compete, the Profitboss eliminates complacency and achieves complete dedication to service. You see it in his team, in their continuing quest for high quality and total customer satisfaction. They know that any shortfall in product quality or deficiency in service is a competitive opportunity. They know that they put their jobs on the line with any such shortfall.

To make profit, the Profitboss has only one objective: to beat the hell out of the competition. He is ruthless in his determination to eliminate them. In a harshly competitive world there is little mercy. If anyone is going to lose a job, it won't be the Profitboss.

TODAY'S STEP

Ask yourself: do you really know who your competitors are? The answer might not be as obvious as it seems. That money in the consumer's pocket: who else is competing for it? If someone wants to go from A to B, who else is competing to take that person there?

Do you really know in what way your company's products/services have the edge over the competition? Why should a customer buy any one particular company's insurance product as opposed to a similar product from another insurance company?

Examine today how you can take action to develop some further edge over your competitors. A competitive attitude is something that has to be applied every single minute of the working day, and every day of the week.

If you haven't thought about 'competitive edge' today, be assured that your competitors have. Don't be complacent. Think 'competition' right now.

REMEMBER

To survive the PROFITBOSS just has to beat the competition.

Design identity

Design is the interface between the customer and the product function

A product often has little value in the marketplace in isolation from its design. Better a sleek elegant automobile than an ugly box on wheels.

Companies express their personality – conservativeness or entrepreneurial flair, self-aggrandisement or customer sensitivity – through all aspects of design.

The company is perceived through its design, is judged by it. What's more, people buy design rather than function. If not, why bother to design a beer can, the dust-jacket of a book or the interior of a restaurant? The beer won't change flavour because of the can's design; the book will read the same, irrespective of the dust-jacket; and the food in the restaurant will taste just as good, whatever the interior design.

The Profitboss is part of the total design. Whether he runs the vehicle maintenance unit or is responsible for product planning he will have an impact on how the company's products and services are perceived by the customer. That's all part of the design.

Design extends beyond the product function to every aspect of the customer interface. Telephonists, receptionists, accounts people, recruiters and nearly every employee are part of the design, part of the totality.

Design extends beyond the product you unpack from the box. It extends to the Profitboss and every member of his team.

TODAY'S STEP

Design something today. Whatever your design, make sure that it integrates with company design and, what's more, contributes to profit.

Don't block your mind to the seeming impossibility of the task. For a start, trace the relationship between your responsibilities and the end-product (or service) perceived by the customer. Now look at that relationship and see if you can design some improvement. (The litter on the floor is just as much a faulty part of the design as the unopenability of the badly designed peanut pack.)

The letter you write is part of your company's design, as is the way the telephonist answers a call. When customers judge a company, they judge the totality, not the basic function.

REMEMBER

The PROFITBOSS is an integral part of the design on profit.

Marketing

Every single employee markets the company

Marketing is all about visibility. Companies fail because no one sees the opportunities in the marketplace and, furthermore, the market doesn't see what the company has on offer.

Markets are dynamic and forever changing. Even in periods of recession the opportunities exist to take a greater market share, to create a new market, to develop a new product or service to meet an unfulfilled need.

No one person or department can resource the company's marketing effort. It must be a total team effort with every single employee contributing as the company's eyes, ears and mouthpiece in the marketplace.

The Profitboss supports this marketing effort and so does his team. When he talks to customers, writes letters, takes telephone calls, walks into a shop, reads a newspaper, he is marketing. When he's out on the street he's totally aware of what's happening to the market, of what the competition is doing, of what customers want. He's looking to see whether his company's products are on display, whether or not people notice them, buy them. That's all part of his marketing effort.

The Profitboss presents himself, his products, his company, his people in the best possible light. That's marketing. He ensures that packaging is neat, addresses correct, initials included. He ensures that deliveries are punctual and accounts paid on time. That's marketing.

For the Profitboss a company's marketing effort is a hundred times *more* than just what the marketing experts do. It is what he and his team do.

TODAY'S STEP

When did you last do any marketing for the company? Today's your chance. Whether you are accounts manager, personnel manager or production manager, think 'marketing'. Don't just leave it to the marketing people.

Think carefully about the next telephone call you receive. The way you present yourself in responding is the way you present the company. That's marketing. Think carefully about the next letter you write. Whatever the letter, and to whomever, it is a marketing letter.

When you take a break at lunch-time, have a look around the local shops. Find out what's happening to your company's products and services and give some feedback to the appropriate people. That's marketing.

And if your friends at the club tell you there's an opportunity to go upmarket, convince your boss of the opportunity and do just that.

REMEMBER

The PROFITBOSS has an eye on the market when others have an eye on themselves.

Publicity

Publicize your products and your people, but never yourself

Publicity is communicating. It is pushing your products, your people and therefore your company in the best possible light.

The Profitboss doesn't need to throw a light on himself: he glows with profit achievement already – and it's obvious for all to see.

Publicity provides ego-trips, pride and satisfaction. It is a positive force which the Profitboss uses both to motivate his customer into buying and his staff into trying.

The Profitboss gets his staff and their profit-achievements into the company newspaper and the local press. If there is an outstanding success, he'll get them on to television and into the national press. It tells his customers, his suppliers and colleagues a lot about his people and the products they are producing. The millionth customer, the millionth unit produced, the 200 per cent sales performance and a major project completed are all worthy of the Profitboss's endeavours to achieve publicity for his team.

Without publicity the team profits less. Without publicity the team will be less motivated to achieve. Publicity provides the reputation for the team and the products they produce and sell. It is the maintenance of that reputation that provides a key motivational force.

Publicity is an important tool for the Profitboss. Even so, the last thing a Profitboss does is get publicity for himself.

TODAY'S STEP

Publicize your team's achievements today. If your team has no achievements to speak of, most likely you are an unspeakably bad manager.

Newspapers (company and local) are always desperate for stories. Don't be frightened of speaking up, don't let those so-called 'publicity professionals' at the centre scare you away. If you really want your customers and staff motivated, feed them some genuine positive publicity today!

Tell the story: a record week, a record month, a record year. They are all worthy of publicity. Don't your staff ever set records? Why not? There's always scope for setting new records. Start today and get some publicity for their achievements. You'll feel much better afterwards.

REMEMBER

The PROFITBOSS publicizes his team, not himself.

Selling

To sell successfully you must have genuine belief in what you are selling

There is nothing wrong with selling except in the way some people do it. The used-car trader, the insurance 'consultant', the door-to-door sales person applying high-pressure techniques have all brought selling into disrepute. They are perceived as 'fast-talking' con-men who are insincere and exploit unwilling customers. They are people who live 'on the surface', living off expenses, living in hotels, aeroplanes and motor cars.

At corporate level it's not much different. The never-ending rounds of golf and cocktail circuits ostensibly develop excellent customer relations but these are effectively no more than a veneer of sincerity in the rude pursuit of the fast sale.

Most sales people are that false that they will only want to know you if they can sell you something. At home they propagate a mythological aura about their secret sales expertise, often no more than the latest gimmicks applied to age-old techniques. There is nothing new about a false smile, a slap on the back, the friendly use of a Christian name or artificial flattery. Sales trainers call it 'body language' or 'positive thinking'.

There might be a thousand methods for closing the deal, but in the end the customers will buy only if they want to buy. The sales person who puts pressure on customers to buy when they don't want to will be out of business tomorrow.

The Profitboss doesn't see selling in that way at all. For a start, he is a believer. He genuinely believes in what he sells. He believes that his company has first-class products and services; he believes in his company. He sells his company and he sells himself, marketing his own deeply held convictions. He believes in putting the customer first and that means meeting their needs before his own. It means straight dealing – dealing based on honesty and openness. Integrity is of the essence in selling.

The Profitboss genuinely cares for his customers and develops sound trusting relationships with them over a long period of time. He doesn't drop them just because they don't buy. He is interested in them as people, not as buyers.

The Profitboss also believes that every single company employee is a sales person, whether on the road calling on clients, or in Accounts processing invoices.

He believes that the secret of successful selling comes from careful preparation and hard work. It comes from taking a genuine interest in and having persistent enthusiasm for the company's products, services and customers.

Successful selling comes from believing.

TODAY'S STEP

Answer these questions:

- Do you genuinely believe that your company's products and services are the best in the marketplace? Why are they best?

- Do you really know your customers?

- Do all your people see themselves as having a selling role?

- Do you and your team seize every possible opportunity to sell?

- Do you work hard to prepare for every sales meeting?

If you can honestly answer 'Yes' to every question, the probability is that you can sell exceptionally well.

REMEMBER

For the PROFITBOSS every minute of the day is a selling opportunity.

Customers

Customer satisfaction is the prime source of job satisfaction

There are hotels which keep you waiting at reception, restaurants that serve you cold coffee, shops which never have what you want in stock, mail-order firms that take three months to deliver the wrong goods. There are thousands of employees (if not millions) who are indifferent to the people who keep them in jobs.

As customers we've all experienced the worst. So many companies still get it wrong. It brings into question the fundamental and obvious belief that one should always put the customer first. Many companies clearly don't. Why is it that the simple act of purchasing something can often be hell? Why is it that so many companies fail on the simple basic of putting the customer first?

The Profitboss puts the customer before himself. For him customer-orientation is synonymous with profit-making. Regarding the customer as all-important is an attitude of mind that he develops and encourages through the organization. It is a key to his selection process, a key to the training he undertakes, a key to his overall process of management. It is a key that he never neglects.

Serving the customer well is a central driving force for the Profitboss and he invests a huge amount of time, effort and resource in getting this right. He develops within his staff a high degree of customer sensitivity and receptivity. He trains his people to identify customer needs clearly and to go out of their way to meet those needs.

Every single person in his organization has a major role to play in pleasing the customer and they know it, and do it.

TODAY'S STEP

Think about your customers, inside and outside the organization. Who are they? Can you put your hand on your heart and say that you and your team are providing a first-class service to them? If not, why not?

Convene your team and spend half a day undertaking a fundamental review of 'customer-service orientation' in your area. Identify at least ten ways of improving it.

Then go and implement the improvements. Do something for your customers today.

REMEMBER

The PROFITBOSS keeps his customers under intensive care.

Contacts

Co-operation and trust can only be established through contact

There is a limit to how much business you can do by remote control. The best business is done with people you know and trust, people who are prepared to co-operate with you and with whom you are prepared to co-operate.

The Profitboss, whatever his job, builds up over the years a wide range of contacts to whom he gives assistance and with whom he exchanges information as well as completes mutually beneficial business deals. He goes to great lengths to maintain these contacts, telephoning them at regular intervals to find out how things are going, to express a genuine interest in their welfare, to see if he can help in any way.

Business thrives on personal relationships. That's why large companies often fail and small companies step in. Large companies grow like dinosaurs and are forever re-organizing. As a result they lose contact with everybody – with their employees, their customers and their suppliers too. Small companies, which rarely re-organize, thrive on personal contacts.

The Profitboss, in developing his contacts, never forgets that the friendly Steven Cook he met at the conference last month might just be the head of purchasing for a major customer in two years' time. He'll follow up the contact, phone Steven, drop by and see him. He'll identify ways in which he can help Steven. Who knows what will come out of the contact? The Profitboss does.

The Profitboss invests time in developing and maintaining personal contact, whether it be internally with the service engineers or people from Accounts, or externally with his customers or potential customers. There's profit in that.

TODAY'S STEP

Prepare a simple 'contact' file with a page for every person and the date when you made the contact. Up date it regularly.

Every month discipline yourself to go through the file and identify at least ten external contacts to phone.

Further discipline yourself to get around your own organization and maintain contact with the people who count, the people who do the real work.

Finally, make sure that you devote sufficient time in December to sending out Christmas cards containing personal messages. The more you send, the better. The ratio of cards sent to cards received is a good measure of 'contact capability'.

REMEMBER

The PROFITBOSS initiates contacts, never waiting for people to contact him.

Selling on

Do your customers a favour! Sell on!

The taxi-driver in Glasgow handed Carole Lacey his card. He sold on. Carole telephoned his taxi service three times that week.

The waiter at Le Coq d'Or asked Nick Thornton whether his guests should have small or large brandies. He sold on: Nick had no option but to order large.

When Hugh Laval cancelled an airline reservation from Boston, the guy at the other end of the telephone went out of his way to identify Hugh's new travel plans. He sold on, securing an alternative reservation.

The Profitboss never leaves a client without fixing the next meeting. He sells on.

The Profitboss teaches his people how to sell the tie with the shirt, the shirt with the suit, the suit with a smile. He gives them scope to do the deal, to become entrepreneurial. He rewards them accordingly. There's profit in that.

Selling on is an attitude of mind, an attitude whereby you do your customers a favour by selling them more than they ask for, and often at a better price than they expected.

TODAY'S STEP

Examine carefully every specific selling interface you and your people have with existing and potential customers. Identify the opportunities for selling on and target for an extra 10 per cent.

If you open your mind to all possibilities, you might surprise yourself (and the rest of the team) with the number of opportunities that exist for selling on.

REMEMBER

The PROFITBOSS gets on by selling on.

Complaints

A complaint is a selling opportunity

Nobody is perfect. Customers are always complaining. The Profitboss seizes each complaint as a selling opportunity, convincing the customer that he really cares. It's an opportunity to eliminate yet another imperfection from the system and improve service further.

Each complaint is followed through with a personal letter or a personal call. The Profitboss is not satisfied until the customer is satisfied. Never will the Profitboss neglect the customer, never will he fail to respond to customer comments, moans and groans. He always tackles the issue head-on, there and then.

Rapid resolution of customer complaints is a matter of life and death for the Profitboss. He cannot afford to lose one single customer. He therefore puts each complaint into intensive care, knowing that nine times out of ten his customers will return even more satisfied.

The Profitboss forbids stereo-typed word-processed responses to complaints. He insists on personal attention every time, no matter how trivial the issue. At best that personal attention will be a personal visit to the customer. Sometimes it will be a personal telephone call within twenty-four hours of receiving a letter. The least he can do is respond immediately with a carefully worded personal letter.

If the customer has taken the trouble to complain (which is far better than not complaining – the Profitboss would never know about lapses in service otherwise), the Profitboss takes the trouble to respond. That response is always positive and constructive, never defensive or full of excuses.

The Profitboss will always investigate the complaint, putting personal time, effort and resource into resolving the issue. He always follows up, if necessary, with a second response to the customer to inform him or her of the corrective action taken.

TODAY'S STEP

If customer complaints pass your desk, ensure that you give them maximum time and personal attention. If they are addressed to your job or you personally, always reply personally, if necessary with an immediate acknowledgement saying that you will investigate. Always follow up with a later letter. Try to telephone the complainant if you can. Even go and visit the person. This will work wonders in terms of future sales.

If customer complaints don't come your way, go down to the Customer Relations Department and chat to the people there. Find out what the customers really think about your products and services. It could just be that you are the indirect cause of the complaint and the action you take has a consequential impact on the customer.

Finally, when resolving a customer complaint, always try to 'sell on' in a discreet and indirect way: 'We look forward to seeing you again, sir/madam. When you do come in, don't hesitate to let me know. I'd welcome your views on our service then;' or 'We are confident that next time you purchase one of our products there will be no problem. Perhaps you'd give a ring and let me know – I'd welcome your feedback.'

REMEMBER

The PROFITBOSS ensures that resolving customer complaints and selling on have first claim on his own personal time and attention.

Prospects

In every person there is the prospect of profit

One never knows when the next encounter will lead to profit. But every encounter brings the prospect of profit.

The person you sit next to on an aeroplane is a prospect. The person who complains about your products is a prospect. The person who reads your article is a prospect. The person who knows a friend of your friend is a prospect. The junior clerk in the Profitboss's team is a prospect. The unsolicited recruitment application is a prospect. A chance encounter in a restaurant is a prospect.

A balls-up by the competition is a prospect. The telephone directory is a prospect, so is the local newspaper. The ink in your pen is a prospect, as is the next telephone number you dial – internally or externally.

The minute you get to work brings some prospect. Every minute of the day is the same.

The prospect is profit. It is always there.

TODAY'S STEP

Open your eyes to the prospects today – the prospects for profit. Set yourself a target of identifying three good prospects for improving profit levels.

When Nelson Lord rings, consider the prospects. Walk along the street, look at the shops. What are the prospects? Go down to the factory floor. Carefully examine what's going on. What are the prospects?

You have to answer. If you don't someone else will.

REMEMBER

The PROFITBOSS never stops prospecting for profit.

Quick Reference Index

John Fenton
How to Sell against Competition £3.99

An inspirational, definitive guide to effective selling based on Jonn
Fenton's unique blend of experience as salesman, communicator and writer,
How to Sell against Competition supplies the key to winning orders and
improving results. The crisp practical advice, always backed up by example,
is designed for immediate application in every branch of selling.

Heinz M. Goldmann
How to Win Customers £3.50

How to Win Customers is not just a book about selling. It is a step-by-step
training course – definitive, practical and complete – on the improvement of
sales techniques. It should be read by everyone concerned with sales and it
can also be used for personal evaluation and improvement, discussion
groups, and for role-playing exercises on sales courses. No one who reads
it can fail to learn from it.

Michael Edwardes
Back from the Brink £3.50

'Essential reading for anyone who struggles to understand the realities of
our commercial condition' ROY HATTERSLEY

'He sees things clearly and simply. He has an exciting story to tell and he
tells it brilliantly' THE DIRECTOR

'In five years he succeeded in transforming BL. Its products are more
reliable and imaginative, its economic performance is better, its factory
efficiency second to none in Europe' THE TIMES LITERARY SUPPLEMENT

'Learn the lessons well' DEREK ROBINSON

John Fenton
The A–Z of Sales Management £2.95

The book for the sales manager. If you are responsible for a sales force,
John Fenton can help you – no matter how successful or experienced you
are – to improve your own and your team's performance. This book covers
the full range of activities and requirements, and includes:

- credit control
- decision making
- expense accounts
- planning and control systems

and much more. Whether you are a marketing manager, managing director
or manager of a small business, this book will help you. And if you've got
ambitions . . .

How to Double Your Profits Within the Year £3.50

John Fenton's unique plan is applicable to all types of business and will
help you to *at least* double your profits within twelve months. You will be
convinced, in the few hours it takes to read this book, that the title's claim
is a modest understatement. The book is an extended memo, written by a
managing director to his team of top managers. To give a few examples, it
shows you how:

- to choose which customers generate profit
- to recruit the right people
- to improve production efficiency
- to price for maximum profit
- to control your sales force

William Kay
Tycoons £2.95

How do tycoons like Robert Maxwell and Sir Terence Conran make their
fortunes? When did they decide to start out on their own? How did they
begin? What attracted them to the competitive, exciting world of business?
And what keeps them at it long after they've made more money than they
could spend in several lifetimes? Do *you* have what it takes?

In this highly stimulating and above all instructive analysis of what makes
top tycoons tick, William Kay, City Editor of *The Times*, charts the careers
of thirteen of Britain's most successful entrepreneurs. In far greater depth
than ever before, they explain to Kay how they got going, they reveal the
secrets behind their continuing success, and they offer priceless advice to
every aspiring tycoon who wants to take the plunge.

'In business, if you are persistent you normally arrive. It's the old tortoise
and hare story. You don't have to be supergood . . .' NOEL LISTER, MFI

David Ogilvy
Confessions of an Advertising Man £3.95
The Classic book on advertising

David Ogilvy is the doyen of advertising. The products he has advertised have been known to millions throughout the world since he started his agency in New York in 1949.

Confessions of an Advertising Man, first published in 1963, was a distillation of all the successful Ogilvy concepts, tactics and techniques – it rapidly became an international bestseller. Now, David Ogilvy has written an updated review of his industry to consolidate this revised edition of *Confessions* – published for the first time in Pan Books.

Confessions is the standard introduction to advertising, written in the bracingly robust style which has become the Ogilvy hallmark. It is the ideal 'how to' guide:

- How to acquire clients and keep them
- How to be a good client
- How to build strong campaigns
- How to write potent copy
- How to make television commercials
- How to rise to the top of the tree

Confessions is required reading for everyone in the advertising industry, from bottom to top.

Graham Mott
Investment Appraisal for Managers £2.95
a guide to profit planning for all managers

Every responsible manager wants a say in how his company uses its
resources. This text provides non-accountants with sufficient financial
knowledge to evaluate profit opportunities and contribute effectively when
investment decisions are made. The clear and uncomplicated treatment is
also geared to the requirements of students on the relevant professional
courses. The author identifies the main assessment techniques, and looks in
detail at yearly cash flows, taxation and effects of inflation, with examples
and case studies.

John Winkler
Pricing for Results £3.95

Bad pricing decisions can ruin the sales prospects of any product, as countless businesses have discovered. John Winkler has used his unique appreciation of the pricing mechanism to win many commercial battles. In *Pricing for Results*, he shows how to win the price war.

Effective pricing skills are crucial in the industrial, consumer and service sectors of any country. The Winkler approach can thus be commended to all finance and sales directors/managers, key account negotiators, general managers and students of marketing.

The Winkler formula explains:

- How to SET prices
- How to PRESENT prices
- How to DISCOUNT prices
- How to NEGOTIATE prices

Bargaining for Results £3.95

Skilful bargaining is a crucial factor in business, especially when money is tight. John Winkler, one of Britain's leading marketing experts, presents the key to effective negotiation – he explains the tactics to adopt and shows when and how to apply them.

The Winkler approach is highly practical, using case histories, illustrations and helpful maxims throughout the text.

Learn how to avoid the traps by following the Winkler formula for successful business negotiation:

- How to cope with difficult customers
- How to apply pressure
- How to obtain the right price
- How to handle monopoly suppliers
- How to deal with bribery

All Pan books are available at your local bookshop or newsagent, or can be ordered direct from the publisher. Indicate the number of copies required and fill in the form below.

Send to: **CS Department, Pan Books Ltd., P.O. Box 40,
Basingstoke, Hants.   RG21 2YT.**

or phone: 0256 469551 (Ansaphone), quoting title, author and Credit Card number.

Please enclose a remittance* to the value of the cover price plus: 60p for the first book plus 30p per copy for each additional book ordered to a maximum charge of £2.40 to cover postage and packing.

*Payment may be made in sterling by UK personal cheque, postal order, sterling draft or international money order, made payable to Pan Books Ltd.

Alternatively by Barclaycard/Access:

Card No. | | | | | | | | | | | | | | | | | |

————————————————————————————————
Signature:

Applicable only in the UK and Republic of Ireland.

While every effort is made to keep prices low, it is sometimes necessary to increase prices at short notice. Pan Books reserve the right to show on covers and charge new retail prices which may differ from those advertised in the text or elsewhere.

NAME AND ADDRESS IN BLOCK LETTERS PLEASE:

....

Name————————————————————————————————

Address—————————————————————————————

————————————————————————————————

————————————————————————————————

————————————————————————————————

3/87